C000090145

HEAD IN THE CLOUDS

A Young
RAF Pilot's Life
in the Late
'30s

GORONWY EDWARDS

Airlife
England

Dedication

This book is dedicated to those who combine the spirit of adventure with a sense of humour, the latter so necessary for the philosophical acceptance of the numerous setbacks which such a lifestyle engenders.

It is also dedicated, with a sense of deep gratitude, to those who have so kindly tolerated and supported the activities of such a person.

Copyright © 1996 Goronwy Edwards

First published in the UK in 1996
by Airlife Publishing Ltd

British Library Cataloguing in Publication Data
A catalogue record for this book
is available from the British Library

ISBN 1 85310 590 2

All rights reserved. No part of this publication
may be reproduced or transmitted in any form or by
any means, electronic or mechanical including photocopying,
recording or by any information storage and retrieval
system, without permission from the Publisher in writing.

Typeset by Hewer Text Composition Services, Edinburgh
Printed in England by St Edmundsbury Press Ltd, Bury St Edmunds, Suffolk

Airlife Publishing Ltd
101 Longden Road, Shrewsbury, SY3 9EB, England

CONTENTS

FOREWORD

by Group Captain H.E. Hopkins, CBE, DFC, AFC, RAF Retd.

In August 1937 I was posted to No. 233 Squadron, a typical Coastal Command squadron of that period. It had only a small nucleus of experienced officers, who had to lick into shape for the forthcoming war a large number of young and newly qualified aircrew.

We were fortunate in having as our Commanding Officer Wing Commander Louis Croke, a dynamic leader determined to have his Squadron on the top line. He breathed a new energy into the Squadron. An ex-naval aviator, he initiated a 'Spring Cruise' on the lines of the Royal Navy's. For the better part of a week the entire Squadron flew around the Coastal Command stations of the UK. Then he set the Squadron a target of a thousand flying hours in a single month, a feat unheard of in those days. And when the Squadron moved to Scotland he imaginatively formed a pipe band.

Shortly after I joined 233 the author arrived, and became a fellow member of 'B' Flight. We flew together on many occasions, including fourteen operational sorties when war broke out. As casualties took their toll I was moved to 'A' Flight, but by this time I was well acquainted with him, and can vouch for the veracity of the incidents which he recalls so vividly.

I well remember one, not recounted in this book, which reflected two of Gron Edwards's many attributes: initiative, and swift reaction. At a somewhat lively mess party our fellow squadron, 224, got a bit uppity, so Gron decided they needed controlling. He collected his flintlock duelling pistols from his quarters, loaded

7

them up with blank charges and let off a few bangs, the room filling with smoke. A rather humourless Flight Lieutenant from 224 ordered him to bed and, when the order was answered by another pair of discharges, escorted him to the door of the mess which led to the quarters.

'Out you go,' said the Flight Lieutenant.

But Gron stood aside and replied respectfully, 'No sir, senior officers first.' Through went the unsuspecting senior officer, whereupon Gron slammed the door, locked him out, reloaded his pistols and set to work again.

It is my pleasure to write this foreword to Gron's instructive and humorous account of those days of long ago, days soon to become so very much more serious, and days which changed the lives of all of us.

UMHLALI,
SOUTH AFRICA

Author's Introduction

Head In The Clouds covers the three years leading up to the outbreak of the Second World War, as seen through the eyes of a young pilot in the Royal Air Force.

Then, the world was different. The British Empire, upon which the sun never set, was already starting to crumble, though we were unaware of it. 'Join The Army And See The World' said the recruiting posters. If you did you probably would. The RAF, with flying accidents in mind, altered the wording somewhat – 'Join The Air Force And See The Next World'.

The nineteen thirties were not perfect: unemployment was high, and social benefits well below today's levels. The gulf between rich and poor was much wider than it is nowadays, and despite the fact that the dictators were already rattling their sabres, the Armed Forces had been badly neglected.

But it was undoubtedly a kinder and less stressful world. The children attending my village school in North Wales walked up to two miles each way from their homes, with never a thought of molestation. Drugs had not arrived, and pensioners weren't kicked to death for the few pounds in their pockets.

The British Empire is much criticised today, few people appreciating that millions, yes *millions*, of the peoples whom we 'held down' would be alive today, with higher standards of living and education, had we carried on with our comparatively benevolent regime, and not handed them over to politicians of their own races, so many of whom have proved to be corrupt and vicious oppressors.

By today's standards of political correctness there will inevitably be an element of 'colonialism' in this account of RAF life in the nineteen thirties. But, knowing no other system, we were, of course, 'colonial'.

The system gave the young men of that generation unparalleled opportunities for adventure, and they made the most of it. As in all things there was a price to pay. When the storm broke upon them in 1939 and 1940 their inadequate numbers had to take the initial brunt of the dictators' onslaught. They suffered grievous losses, but they held the fort long enough for Britain to rearm.

However, that was later. After soloing before my eighteenth birthday in the biplanes of that era, the RAF opened up a whole new world to me, and to others of my generation whose aspirations took them into the air. It was a great deal of fun.

CHAPTER 1

THE FLEDGLING

In 1903 the Wright brothers made the first heavier-than-air flight. Six years later Blériot flew the English Channel, and ten years after that Alcock and Brown flew the North Atlantic. Six years again after that a less distinguished flight was made by a 'barnstormer' in South Wales, one of the many ex-World War One pilots who travelled the country flying out of farmers' fields, offering joy rides at five shillings a time, or seven and sixpence if you wanted to loop the loop.

They lived simply and frugally, these barnstormers, their outfits consisting as often as not of a mechanic, an Army surplus bell tent in which they both slept, and a truck which served as a travelling workshop. Their aircraft were chiefly Avro 504s, old biplane trainers modified to carry two passengers or, in some cases, four. Rugged and reliable, the 504s could operate from any field of reasonable size. These men flew around the country, advertising in the local papers, nailing their posters to telegraph poles and field gates, and flying low over the towns to drum up trade. It was one such poster that had caught the eye of my two older brothers. They had dashed home and persuaded my father to buy them flights. Fortunately, I had intercepted the trio as they left the house, and demanded equal treatment.

'You can't fly,' snorted my eldest brother. 'You're only seven.'

I protested so vigorously at the flawed argument that my mother, despairing at the street row now raging on the doorstep, told my father to take me too.

It took only five minutes to get washed and changed into the best suit that one wore for all such occasions in the twenties, and we set off on our two-mile walk to Dick Vaughan's farm, passing poster after poster advertising Captain Rumford's five-shilling joy rides – 'Only seven and six to loop the loop'. When that old Avro rumbled across the field and bounced gently into the air I knew that flying would have to be my life!

Another opportunity to fly had arisen six years later, when Sir Alan Cobham's Flying Circus had arrived at a farm five miles away. A much more sophisticated affair than Captain Rumford's, the six Avro 504s were dominated by an airliner that could carry ten people. But this time my mother, now widowed, couldn't afford the money. I still walked the five miles to the air show, and stood enviously on the sidelines as people more fortunate than myself took to the air. 'There are still four seats left in the Siddeley Mongoose Avros for the last flight of the day,' came over the public address system. Though none of those seats were for me, I stayed until the very last machine landed before starting on the journey home.

Some day, I vowed, I'd get into the air again, but in the meantime I had to content myself with flying my Warneford model aircraft. Its fuselage was a single stick of wood, its wings a silk-covered open framework and its motive power twisted strands of rubber. By winding the propeller backwards through the recommended 200 turns, plus a few dozen extra that the instruction manual had warned would over-stress the model, it flew for about thirty seconds.

Flying this model one day, I became aware that a faint droning that had been part of the background for some time had now grown rapidly in volume, and a Hart light bomber of the Royal Air Force appeared over the hill and slid down into the shallow valley. The roar of its 500 horsepower engine filled the air as it swept overhead in a steeply banked turn, then died away as the pilot cut the throttle and glided towards the field, as though to land. The big biplane, with the wind sighing gently in its bracing wires, came low over the hedge, and I waited expectantly for this heaven-sent opportunity to see a powerful military aircraft close up, and for the chance to talk to its demi-god of a pilot. But he aborted the landing, went round again and made another attempt, then yet a third, before deciding that the field was too small for his forced landing.

He flew away over the hill. Disappointed beyond measure, I walked back to the village. But that pilot had achieved something: he'd made me realise that the time for daydreaming about flying was over and that I would have to do something about it.

My mother certainly couldn't afford to train me as an Imperial Airways pilot – they said that it took about a thousand pounds – but maybe there was another way into flying. My eldest brother, by sheer hard work they said, had won a scholarship to university, so maybe I could do the same. As Cambridge was the only university with a course in aeronautical engineering it looked as though Cambridge it was going to be. To the astonishment of my teachers I started to work at school, and to get rid of the despairing '*yet he has the ability*' type of report that my headmaster had written about last term's efforts.

I was spurred on by the rapid developments in aviation which were being increasingly reported in the papers. In 1928 Bert Hinkler had flown from England to Australia in fifteen days, a third of the time taken by the P&O liners to sail the distance. Three years later Amy Johnson had cut Hinkler's time to nine days! Within a few years Alex Henshaw had flown to South Africa and back in some incredibly short time. The world was shrinking fast.

Well motivated, I beavered away and matriculated, two years later gaining my Higher School Certificate, the chief result being that my grandfather, in view of the financial obstacles still in the way of my getting into Cambridge, said he could get me a position as an articled clerk to a chartered accountant. Mr Roberts wore bat-winged stiff collars with his pin-striped suit, the only type of suit he was ever seen in, come sunshine, hail, snow or sleet. He was worthy and dull, and enthusiastic about figures, but only of the non-female sort. A lifetime in his office was the knell of doom. But it was, of course, a job, and not to be sniffed at in the hungry thirties.

And then the advertisement appeared in one of my flying magazines: 'Applications will be considered for Short Service Commissions in the General Duties (Flying) Branch of the Royal Air Force.' It went on to give the educational requirements, which were well within my grasp, and my age was just right too, not less than seventeen and three quarters. After absorbing the details which they sent to me by post it wasn't too difficult winning over my mother, as she'd lived flying with me ever since that joyride ten years before.

But there was a far more difficult hurdle to overcome. Uncle Dick, my mother's brother, had become the titular head of the family since my father's death. Though a kindly man, he was inclined to bark, and to make authoritative statements which were not expected to be contested. It was said of him that he didn't suffer fools gladly, which put me at an immediate disadvantage, as I was a shy and retiring character inclined to let people walk all over me in arguments. My mother warned that he would probably veto the project. I approached the presence and laid the proposition before him.

'Fly!' snorted he. 'You mean fly for a *living*?'

'God, what a start!' I thought. But it gave me a lead, because from the moment of shaking the dust of North Wales off my feet I would be self-supporting, which would help the tottering finances of the family no end. This self-sufficiency appealed to me immensely, as I was fed up with having to wear my older brothers' cast-off clothes, especially the shoes.

Shoes had now replaced boots as the accepted form of footwear, and while I had found it quite feasible to wear boots a size or so too large, as the laces round your ankles held them securely in place, an oversize pair of shoes was another kettle of fish altogether, and there were many embarrassing moments at school when a shoe would fall off despite my attempts to hold it on by curling my toes down. My loathing of reach-me-down shoes gave me the courage to return to the attack, but I was forestalled.

'Anyway, it's too dangerous,' continued Uncle Dick. 'Think of Willie Bailey.'

Silently, I cursed the late Willie Bailey. He had bought himself a war-surplus Avro, but had looped the loop once too often and killed himself. I had often gazed at the wreckage of his machine, stacked away at the back of the Bailey family's garage.

'No, you must be mad to want to fly for a living.'

Desperate, I played a timorous ace. Uncle Dick was known locally as 'Mad Dick', having earned the title many years before. A graduate of the Toad School of Motoring, he was addicted to powerful American cars which he drove flat out for most of the

time, scattering the Welsh peasantry like chaff before him. To
him pedestrians belonged to those two religious categories, the
quick and the dead, and when Mad Dick was around people
took the hint and sprinted for cover. When Uncle Dick opined
that anyone who wanted to fly for a living must be mad the 1936
equivalent of the crunch had come for me. He had to be beaten
on this one or I'd be a penguin to the end of my days. What was
sauce for the goose was sauce for the gander. I looked my fellow
madman firmly in the eye.

'There are quite a few people in the village who think it a darned
sight safer in the cockpit of an aeroplane than riding round as a
passenger in that Studebaker of yours,' I retorted, appalled at my
rashness, but also distressed at the high-pitched squeak in which
my protest had been delivered.

Mad Dick took his pipe from his mouth, inhaled long and deep
and went purple. But as my knees shook the purple diminished to
red, then merely to bright pink. He put his pipe back in his mouth
and grunted like a wounded boar; it looked like the moment to
put the boot in.

'Still like omelettes, Uncle Dick? I asked insolently.

Some weeks before he'd swept round the corner of a narrow
lane, and a farmer's wife walking to market had sacrificed twelve
dozen eggs rather than her life as well. As she clambered out of
the quickthorn hedge Uncle Dick went into his near-miss routine,
dusting her down, asking after the children, and offering the going
rate plus fifty per cent for the eggs. He took possession of those
which had survived, and it was rumoured that he had lived on
omelettes for a fortnight after the incident.

But you couldn't keep Uncle Dick down for long. Looking at
me with something less than affection he produced his ace.

'But what do you do at the end of your four years' Active List
service, when you will be flung out on to the Reserve for six
years?' he asked. 'You'll have no job. There are still an awful lot
of unemployed, you know.'

'I'll have my gratuity of three hundred pounds, all the money
that I will save during my four years' service' (that would have
been good for a laugh had either of us known it) 'and there are
correspondence courses. When I come out in 1940 it'll just be in

time to go to Cambridge and start my aeronautical engineering course.'

Mad Dick was clearly impressed with my foresight.

'Oh all right, you'd better apply I suppose. But there's this civil war in Spain, and I'm sure Hitler's spoiling for a European war – he's got his eye on Austria and Czechoslovakia. And his Luftwaffe is streets ahead of the Air Force in numbers, you know.'

'That's why the RAF is expanding, so it needs pilots. We mean to stop him.'

Uncle Dick was a kindly man, and forebore to cast any doubts on my contribution towards this blocking move, merely remarking, as he signed the form as my guardian, 'Yes, I *still* like omelettes. Look after yourself.'

My interview and medical were successful, and early in October 1936 I travelled by rail to Northampton where at Sywell, a few miles out of the town, Brooklands Aviation had a flying school for the initial training of aspiring RAF pilots. We were still civilians, so if we did not show an aptitude for flying we could be thrown off the course to return to civilian life without all the rigmarole that dismissal from a fighting service entailed. The survivors would go on to the glory of a King's Commission in the Royal Air Force.

We were split up into two groups, one of which flew while the other did ground lectures in Theory of Flight, Airmanship, Meteorology, Engines, Navigation and so on. The big thrill of the first day was drawing our flying kit, the chief item of which was the Sidcot suit, which was a head-to-foot overall of heavy, windproof cotton, with a detachable teddy-bear lining which could be removed for warm-weather flying. Fleece-lined flying boots reaching halfway up the calf, helmets, goggles, Gosport tubes, earpieces and, an act of apparently prodigal generosity, *three* pairs of gloves completed the outfit. We soon found that these gloves were a necessity. The inner pair were expensive treble-layer silk, over which we pulled a pair of rough fibre gloves, topping them with impressive leather gauntlets which came halfway to the elbow. Despite all this kit the biting cold of that winter was to penetrate all the layers I wore.

We drew our parachutes, then went to the tailor to have our helmets fitted with the earpieces for the Gosport tubes, which were flexible metal tubes, half an inch in diameter, running down from each ear to be plugged in to the socket of the voice tube running forward to the instructor's cockpit, where it ended in his mouthpiece, so that anything he said was conveyed directly to your ears through six feet of tubing. Conversely, the pupil's mouthpiece tube ended at the instructor's earpieces. The quality of voice reproduction was poor by modern standards, and it was complicated, in my case, by the fact that I had been 'fitted' with a helmet at least two sizes too large, so that the slipstream in our open cockpits roared and whistled between my cheeks and the loosely flapping helmet and made the interpretation of my instructor's words of wisdom a difficult matter.

Whereas *I* thought he was doing his party-piece imitation of Donald Duck, *he* thought he had a half-wit on his hands, and relations were strained after we landed from the first trip. The second was more successful as I'd stuffed a couple of handkerchiefs in the crown of my helmet and another beneath the chin-strap to take up some of the slack, and this reduced the helmet-flapping business and so made my instructor sound less like cartoon wildfowl. 'Jerks' Ayling was, in fact, an extremely nice man – calm, reassuring and kindly all the time, and I remember him with affection.

This helmet was my first introduction to the more tortuous side of service life, the 'usual channels' and so on. My complaint to the storekeeper about its fit had been countered with the statement that, as a civilian, he could do nothing about Air Force property that had already been used. I came back with the fact that *he* had measured me for the damned thing and that it was his job to ensure a perfect fit, whereupon he launched into a dissertation of what exactly would be required to reverse the decision. It appeared that it would take the personal intervention of the Chief of the Air Staff, Marshal of the Royal Air Force Lord Trenchard, KG, KCB, DSO, MC, DFC etc.

'My hands are tied,' the storekeeper cried, a highly inaccurate statement as he was waving them in the air as he spoke.

I gave up, and walked across to the East Midlands Flying Club, where I forked out for a well-fitting helmet.

'Far superior to the RAF issue,' said their salesman.

He was quite wrong: service flying equipment was first class. Despite this, as I was constitutionally susceptible to cold, even the three layers of gloves could not keep my fingers from freezing in that chilly winter of 1936. As the pain grew I would, if I was flying solo, shout into the slipstream the worst obscenities I knew as I beat my hands on my knees to get some sort of circulation going. If I was flying under Jerks's instruction, however, the blasphemies had to be silent, so weren't half as effective.

But if the drawing of my flying kit on the first day had been a thrill, the second day hit the jackpot. I sat spellbound in the back cockpit of a Tiger Moth and listened to my instructor in the front going through the starting drill.

'Switches off, petrol on, suck in,' called Jerks.

The ground engineer pulled the propeller over a few staccato half-turns.

'Contact,' called Jerks, and flipped the magneto switches upwards.

The engineer swung the propeller, which jerked through a quarter of a revolution before the Gipsy engine rasped into life and spun it into invisibility. As the blast of cold October air stung my cheeks I knew that my dream was coming true.

I went solo just before my eighteenth birthday, and a month later an RAF Flight Lieutenant from the Central Flying School at Upavon flew in to check our progress. He appeared, like a god, in a Hart. The 525 horsepower biplane looked enormous after the delicacy of our little 120 horse Tigers. Everything was big and impressive, the wing bracings looking more like steel rods than wires. The deep-sectioned wings, with their taut linen fabric painted in the standard yellow of the RAF training aircraft – 'Yellow Perils' they were called by the front-line squadrons – looked as though they could lift a ton weight into the air, and they could nearly do that. The gleaming aluminium panels of the nose concealed a Rolls-Royce Kestrel engine of incredible reliability, and you had to climb up three steps before you could even swing your leg over the coaming to get into the front cockpit. It was a lot of aeroplane, and a great incentive to do well on our initial flying course.

Towards the end of the course the constitutional crisis leading to the abdication of King Edward VIII surfaced. It came as a complete surprise to the people of Britain, as hitherto the BBC and the papers had voluntarily suppressed all news of the King's liaison with Mrs Simpson. As the drama rapidly approached its climax the basic feeling of the country was the unthinkability of a twice-divorced American socialite becoming even the morganatic consort of the King. Popular as the King was, this was one thing he couldn't have, and behind the sadness and the sympathy for him was the disappointment that he could contemplate ditching the heritage of Britain to become, who knew, perhaps the third divorced husband of Wallis Simpson. Later, on 10 December 1936, his abdication broadcast stunned a nation who thought that he would pull back at the last moment, as social standards, though deteriorating, had not been eroded to that extent. *Vitai Lampada*, though written four decades earlier, was still not a bad code to live by. We felt that Mrs Simpson, certainly, had not played the game. The shy and retiring Duke of York was forced into the job, but obviously had great support from his vivacious wife, the former Lady Elizabeth Bowes-Lyon.

In the meantime we continued to learn to fly. The survivors of the Sywell course went on to the RAF depot at Uxbridge for a fortnight's disciplinary and drill training, during which we were commissioned into the RAF as Acting Pilot Officers on Probation. We gathered, from our drill sergeants, that there was no lower form of animal life in the service. They voiced humiliating public assessments of our ability at square-bashing without being insubordinate in any way by simply adding the suffix 'Sir' at the end of each stream of insults. Chastening though it was when you were the target, I must say that I found it thoroughly enjoyable when someone else was copping it, and we had many a laugh, to the secret delight of the drill sergeant who had, nevertheless, to keep his aloof position and roar 'Silence in the ranks.' 'Gentlemen' only as an afterthought.

Our religious welfare was taken care of during one of our many lectures on service customs and procedures. On one of the forms we filled in we stated, among other things, our religion. In those politically incorrect days of Empire it was simplest to be Church of England, as the C of E Church Parade was usually fully catered for on the spot, so was the soonest completed, after which you could get down to the papers and your lunchtime beer in peace. Obscure sects, of which there seemed to be a few, often had to make long journeys in the back of a three-ton truck for their spiritual salvation.

We now drew our £50 uniform allowance, and were informed of the three approved military tailoring firms, all of whom presented us with their price lists. We were relieved to see that they could kit us out at sums varying from £49–19–3 to £49–19–6, leaving enough over for half a pint of beer. But the lists omitted to mention that only one of each item was included in the offers, and you can't get very far socially with just one collar to your only shirt and one pair of socks, so we all had to spend at least £60. This was no problem as, in the genteelest possible way, the salesmen introduced us to the hire-purchase system, still in its infancy.

'If you would like to sign this form, sir, for one pound a month, or for more should you wish, we will forward it to your bankers – Cox and Kings I presume, sir? Yes, I'm sure it is,' he continued, implying that anyone not banking there was beneath consideration.

As five bob a week was all that the kitty would stand I signed my pound-a-month order, and started a long association with Gieves. Their shop in Bond Street, before it was destroyed by the Luftwaffe in 1941, was a militarian's delight. In glass cases were miniature figures eighteen inches high, in the uniforms of all branches of the services, and the moment you entered you felt a part of British history. The forebears of the men represented by those midget figures had fought in all the wars from Cromwell onwards. Our figurines had flown their frail biplanes in the Great War of 1914–18, taking the war to the enemy behind the German lines, and having to struggle back to safety against the prevailing westerly winds. And without parachutes, too.

In such an atmosphere you usually ended up ordering more kit than you needed, the bills mounting proportionately. In fact when, some four years later, Winston Churchill pronounced his immortal words about the Battle of Britain that 'Never in the field of human conflict was so much owed by so many to so few', those of us not entirely clued up thought that he was referring to the amounts we all owed to our military tailors.

At Uxbridge I caught a dose of 'flu so missed out, among other things, on learning how to salute correctly, so for some time my salutes were floppy caricatures of the real thing, and a matter of despair to my seniors. However, a bonus of my time in bed was the updating of all the amendments to the two official publications that were supposed to dominate our service careers – *The King's Regulations and Air Council Instructions for the Royal Air Force* (usually known as *King's Regs* or *KR*) and the *Manual of Air Force Law*. Both were massive tomes, and were subject to continuous amendment by the Legal Branch in their efforts to plug holes in the system through which ingenious miscreants had slipped in the past, or might possibly do in the future. Every officer was given the two volumes, and the torrent of amendments which flowed out had to be incorporated into every copy. Small alterations meant just crossing out a few words and writing new ones above them; larger ones entailed crossing out whole paragraphs and sticking the replacements in with glue and, after a few dozen of these had been incorporated, the books became so thick that they would not shut.

Ingenuity could be applied by the originators of the intermediate sized amendments. By juggling, they could insert little 'for X read Y' quickies, thus saving space, so that they would be that much nearer their OBEs. The discipline of the service was built round the complete understanding of *King's Regs* and the *Manual of Air Force Law*, and it was a pronounced failing of the Short Service officer that he failed lamentably to absorb either of them. He'd joined the RAF to fly, not to become a legal wallah.

A third publication, and one that gave me enormous pleasure, was the *RAF Pocket Book*. This was straight out of a modern Outward Bound course, but twenty times better, being in the style of Baden Powell, Rudyard Kipling and Fennimore Cooper. Sadly, I no longer have it, but it gave advice on every possible contingency which could possibly face we upholders of the British Empire. It refreshed us on the Morse code and on zogging – the semaphore-type arm-signalling system used between open-cockpit aircraft before we had radio intercom. Should you fly over a ship of the Royal Navy displaying flags with crisses and crosses, and stars and bars, and stripes in all directions, page 34 would tell you whether the ship was about to sink with all hands or whether the captain had just had a blitz on his crew's personal hygiene. You'd force-landed in Mesopotamia? Remove the magneto inspection cover from the Jupiter engine and use it as a heliograph mirror. It told you how to light a fire with damp wood, using your last match for the purpose or, if you hadn't even got that, to break a bottle and use it as a burning glass. You were living under canvas? It told you how to pitch your tent, and how to discourage ants from getting into your kit. You had been shot down by Waziri tribesmen firing muzzle-loading Jezails that they'd loaded a couple of Ramadans ago? You wished to retain your capability of fathering children? In that case turn to page 213 for an example of a ghoolie-chit. It told you how to cook a lizard. It was all there. For the romantics of the last days of Empire the *RAF Pocket Book* was a source of endless delight.

One aspect of my 'flu was that while my companions were taking the Loyal Oath to King Edward VIII in the mess anteroom, I was lying in my barrack-room sickbed, so didn't take part in the ceremony. I never swore allegiance to the Crown, so it's not beyond the bounds of possibility that had I subsequently defected to the Russians there would have been no legal grounds for my prosecution as a traitor. I never exercised the rather dodgy prerogative, though.

It took quite a time for the administrative wheels to clank, and for our written commissions to arrive. When they did there was a new king on the throne, and we were again living in barrack huts, as the mess at our Flying Training School had been recently burned to the ground. A few of us lay on our beds, reading the fascinating documents. A confirmed traditionalist, even at the age of eighteen, I revelled in its archaic seventeenth-century style and punctuation:

> George VI by the Grace of God, OF GREAT BRITAIN, IRELAND AND THE BRITISH DOMINIONS BEYOND THE SEA, KING, DEFENDER OF THE FAITH, EMPEROR OF INDIA, &C.
> To our trusty and well beloved Goronwy Edwards Greeting:
> We reposing especial Trust and Confidence in your Loyalty, Courage, and good Conduct, do by these Presents Constitute and Appoint you to be an Officer in Our Royal Air Force from the Twenty-first day of December 1936. You are therefore carefully and diligently to discharge your Duty as such in the rank of Acting Pilot Officer or in such higher Rank as We may from time to time

hereafter be pleased to promote or appoint you to, of which a notification will be made in the *London Gazette*, and you are at all times to exercise and well discipline in their Duties both the inferior Officers and Airmen serving under you and use your best endeavours to keep them in good Order and Discipline . . .

McCall's customarily critical voice intruded from the next bed.

'You know,' he announced to the barrack room, 'KG Six is up the pole here. There *is* nothing inferior in the RAF to an Acting Pilot Officer on Probation, so how the hell can we discipline them?'

'Put a sock in it, you bolshie bastard.'

I continued reading:

And We do hereby Command them to Obey you as their superior Officer and you to observe and follow such Orders and Directions as from time to time you shall receive from Us, or any your superior Officer, according to the Rules and Discipline of War, in pursuance of the Trust hereby reposed in you.

Given at Our Court, at Saint James's the Seventeenth day of August 1937 in the First Year of Our Reign.

By His Majesty's Command.

Signed . . .

As the course at Uxbridge drew to a close we drew our camp kits, which contained a folding bed, wash basin-cum-bath, ground sheet/cape, camp stool and all the items of camp gear needed when under canvas. The only active service areas for the RAF in those days were the North-West Frontier of India and Mesopotamia. In both these areas the RAF kept the peace at a fraction of the cost needed when the Army had had to mount ground campaigns against warring tribesmen.

In India the squadrons flew battered old Wapiti biplanes over the most frightful Himalayan territory, with not a hope of a successful forced landing if an engine failed or if rifle fire from the ground brought them down. Indeed, it was often felt that to die in the crash was preferable to baling out by parachute and being handed over to the tribal women for torture, which always ended in castration.

In Waziristan the Fakir of Ipi's insurrection had started just after we joined the course at Sywell, and it was now in full swing in the typical complicated style of the North-West Frontier. The Mahsud and Tori Khel tribesmen hated each other only slightly less than they did the British, and had numerous differences with the Fakir himself. But these active service areas gripped the imagination. One wore the enormous solar topee for protection against the sun, not to mention the spine pad which some imaginative doctor had thought up to protect the spinal column from solar attack. The thought of living under canvas quickened the pulse. The King's peace had to be maintained in the outposts of Empire. One would, indeed, need one's *RAF Pocket Book.*

It was to be eight years before I used my camp kit, in Burma in 1944, and it turned out to be as well designed for its purpose as our flying kit was. For a year I lived with nothing else and, when we eventually got to Rangoon and lived in abandoned houses, we were not half as comfortable as we had been with our camp kits and forty-pounder tents. Biggles and his contemporaries had done a good job on our equipment.

The Uxbridge disciplinary course ended, and we all dispersed for Xmas leave before going on to our Service Flying Training Schools. Back at home the older members of the family seemed unable to grasp the fact that, despite my tender years, I was a fully qualified pilot with fifty flying hours under my belt, and that I had my foot on the first rung of the ladder that was to lead to my eventual rank of Marshal of the Royal Air Force. It was a pity that they'd stuck the 'Acting' and 'On probation' on to my already lowly Pilot Officer status; it made it that much further to have to climb.

'Do they ever let you touch the controls, dear?' an aunt asked.

'Will they ever let you go up alone?' queried another.

'And isn't it awfully dangerous?' quavered an obscure acquaintance.

'And you're not wearing your uniform, dear. How disappointing!' I gave up. Maybe they'd cotton on some day.

CHAPTER 2

SAWDUST DOESN'T FLY

E arly in the new year of 1937 I reported to No. 10 Flying
    Training School, at Tern Hill in Shropshire, to join the
    Junior Term. I was impressed with my first glimpse of an RAF
flying station. The Expansion Scheme was gathering momentum,
and already three of the enormous 'C' type hangars had been built.
An airfield six times the size of Sywell's stretched greenly into the
distance, and modern barrack blocks for the airmen abounded.
The Officers' Mess, however, had burned to the ground a few
months before, so we were to live in a wooden-hut mess and sleep
in wooden barrack blocks, about twenty to a room.

I did not like barrack-room life, with its complete lack of
privacy. If you were tired and went to bed early some clowns
would probably come in hell-raising at an unearthly hour, and
as much noise could arise from other wrathful sleepers as from
the revellers. Doors would slam, or be left open for the January
winds to sweep in, people shouted, quarrels broke out and I came
to the conclusion that a quiet kip-down in Piccadilly Circus would
have been bliss compared to living in close communion with a
bunch of flying types. On the other hand one did get to know
one's companions quicker. Anyway, this was *it*. We were to fly the
fabulous Hart at last.

With a top speed of 184 miles an hour the Hart, when introduced
in 1930, had staggered the Air Force by being ten miles an hour
faster than the current fighter, the Bulldog. Capable of lifting two
crew and a thousand pounds of bombs, guns and ammunition, it
ruined the annual air defence exercises for two years, until a faster
fighter could be produced to catch it. It was a well conceived aircraft
that *looked* right. In the Junior Term we were to repeat all that we

had done on our little Tiger Moths at Sywell, but on these powerful 525 horsepower machines, and they caused us some problems at first. When that growling Krestel engine delivered its full power the torque swung the Hart firmly to the left, and one needed to apply plenty of right rudder to counteract it.

'Edwards', came the patient Scottish voice of Flying Officer Hamilton, my instructor, as I took a dirty dive towards the left-hand corner of the aerodrome for the second time running, 'prevention is better than cure. Don't start with your rudder central and put your right foot forward as the swing develops, put on right rudder *before* you open the throttle and progressively take it off as you gather speed.'

Using this system I managed to clamber into the air reasonably well, and brought the Hart to earth in one piece. Thereafter, I had no further problems with the take-off.

Three trips later I was introduced to the recovery from the spin. Much as I loved the air, I concluded that only the mentally deranged could possibly like their first spin. As the speed dies away the aircraft starts to wallow, then it shudders, and *then* comes the God-awful bit. The nose drops like a plummet, your stomach rises up, and a gigantic hand takes hold of the aircraft and whirls it into mad, gyratory revolutions as you dive vertically earthwards. It just wasn't done to scream in terror, of course, and neither could you clutch the sides of the cockpit in your panic, as the instructor insisted that you use both hands to fly the machine. Eventually, of course, the machine obeyed your input to the controls, and regained a semblance of normal flight.

'Good fun, what, Edwards?' came down the Gosport tubes after my first spin.

'Oh, *rather*, sir. Frightfully good. Dashed good show and all that.'

Lying hound!

One got used to it, of course. Later on, in fact, to enjoy it.

Forced landing practice, in case the engine conked, was genuine fun on the other hand. The instructor would close the throttle on you and say 'Okay, your engine's cut. Set her down in the best field you can find.' These training forced landings were done in the vicinity of one of several fields which were rented from local farmers for the purpose. We approached, as though to land, and if grazing animals scattered, well that's what the farmer was paid for. As you came low over the hedge and your instructor assessed that (1) you would have made it or (2) that you wouldn't, you opened up the throttle and flew away. Many of the animals became so blasé about the whole business that even five hundred snarling horsepower hurtling ten feet above them wouldn't persuade them to lift their heads from the serious business of grazing, or persuade them to move an inch. If one had had to do a genuine forced landing in such a field there would have been a fair amount of scrap metal and lamb chops strewn around at the end of it, plus the odd beefsteak.

'Your engine has failed,' said Hamilton as he closed the throttle on me one day. 'Set her down in a suitable field.'

He'd certainly chosen an awkward spot, as none of the familiar fields was in sight. Maybe there'd be some better ones hidden under the lower wing. I turned the Hart and saw one that I thought I could get her down in.

'Have you chosen your field yet?' queried Hamilton.

'Yes sir, the L-shaped one with a clump of trees on the easterly hedge. The smoke from that cottage chimney shows the wind along the long arm of the L.'

'Very well, set her down and remember to land well into the field. In a forced landing it's better to hit the far hedge slowly than to undershoot and hit the near hedge at high speed. Treat this as the real thing, Edwards. Land it.'

What fun!

The Hart, with the wind soughing gently in its bracing wires, sank earthwards in that comfortable, floaty way of the biplane with its low wing loading.

'That's fine, Edwards. Now I want you to imagine that this field is only half its length. Do you think you could drop it just over the hedge in a short-field landing?'

'If I side-slip off some of my excess height I could do it, sir.'

'Then do it.'

I ruddered the nose to the right, dropped the left wing in the controlled skid of the side-slip and the ground juddered rapidly nearer. At the moment I judged to be correct I centralised the

27

controls, the Hart slipped into smooth flight again, and we just cleared the hedge. I set her down, to rumble and bump over the uneven field, the brakes hard on.

'Good,' said Hamilton. 'Now I don't want the engine to stall, so open the throttle a trifle and keep the brakes on all the time.'

As I trod obediently on the toe pedals I was surprised to see Hamilton throw off his straps and get out of the aircraft. He stood in the steps alongside my cockpit and said, 'Have you got a handkerchief?'

'Yes, thank you all the same, sir.'

'A clean one?'

Well, he'd never find out, would he?

'I'd like to borrow it.'

Odd, but you don't argue with an officer senior to yourself, especially when he's daft enough to force-land in a smallish field just to borrow your handkerchief. I handed over what turned out to be quite a clean one, eminently suitable for the august nose of my instructor. As he took it he barked, 'I said keep the brakes on.'

I must have eased the pressure on the brakes, as the Hart was trickling forward. I stabbed down on the toe pedals, the tail rose fractionally into the air, then settled down with a bump.

'Now keep her like that.'

He climbed to the ground, walked away and stooped down for a while. Peculiar, I mused. He rose to his full height, walked with downcast eyes, stooped yet again and seemed to sweep his hands across the surface. Odd, I thought. Maybe he's a member of some obscure religious cult – he came of a long line of military men. Maybe his grandfather had converted to Islam in India, or something. He repeated the process, always with downcast eyes, but the noise of the engine prevented me from overhearing the incantations which he was undoubtedly uttering as he carried on with his exotic rites.

The engine temperature was rising, so I wound out the radiator to its full extent and wondered how long I was going to be stuck in an undersize field with a superior officer of suspect mental stability. My feet were tiring from having to keep the brake pedals pressed and, despite the radiator's being fully out, the needle of the temperature gauge continued its remorseless rise. Before he'd set off on his weird caper Hamilton had given me instructions to keep the engine running fast enough so that it didn't stall. It was good advice, as the Kestrel engine was so powerful that it took two men with low-geared winding handles to get it started. But the temperature was still rising, and I thought of easing back the throttle a bit. But if I overdid it and stalled the engine not only would I incur Hamilton's wrath, but I would be stuck with a task that normally required the strength of two men – that of winding the big engine until it fired, with Hamilton swanning it in the cockpit just flipping switches on and off, like pilots the world over. No, blow it, the engine would just have to stay hot.

However, eventually it looked as though the gods had been placated as Hamilton, carrying a bulging handkerchief in one hand, approached the one he'd laid on the ground, picked it up, and walked back to the Hart as though on eggs. Somewhat awkwardly he clambered up the steps let into the side of the Hart and held on by hooking his elbows over the coaming.

'Edwards,' he said, 'I want a smooth, gentle take-off, and an equally good landing: slip her on to the deck in a real daisy-cutter. I don't want any of these mushrooms broken.'

'Mushrooms sir?'

'Yes, mushrooms. D'you think I'd leave a valuable aircraft in charge of an Acting Pilot Officer – er, still On Probation, aren't you? Yes, thought as much – unless I had a very good reason. My God, look at that radiator temperature! Get it down, man, get it down.'

'Can't sir, the radiator's fully out.'

'Oh, hell, is it?' In a more conciliatory tone.

'Yes, sir. Er, are they particularly *good* mushrooms?'

'Good! This is the best mushroom field in the whole of Shropshire. Now don't forget that pansy landing.'

He climbed carefully into the back cockpit, and I taxied to the leeward end of the field before giving the Hart full throttle against locked brakes. Releasing them, we bumped across the grass, cleared the far hedge by ten feet, and got into the air. As the radiator temperature came back into the green Hamilton came on the line again.

'You'll have to log the whole time of the trip as flying time, of

29

course; don't deduct our ground time. Put down "Forced landing practice" and "Use of the Mixture Control at medium altitudes". That'll account for the extra time. Not that anyone minds as long as you're not *seen* doing it.

'And while we're on the subject of extra-curricular activities I don't mind, within reason, what you get up to in the air when you're flying solo as long as you bear two things in mind. One you already know – don't be seen doing it. The other is much more important. Whatever you get up to in the air don't, for God's sake, hit the ground while doing it.'

Back at Tern Hill I landed the Hart like thistledown.

'Right Edwards,' said Hamilton, 'here's half a dozen mushrooms. Get the mess steward to cook them with your bacon and eggs for breakfast.'

I felt that the RAF lifestyle was going to suit me.

An aesthetic pleasure for me when doing aerobatics in the Hart was its gravity-feed petrol tank up in the top wing. An air vent opened from the top of this, and when you did a slow roll, a steady stream of petrol would flow out of this, to be immediately vaporised into a snow-white plume streaming away below your head. It was a very pretty sight and, if you held the aircraft on its back for some time, you could get rid of quite a deal of taxpayers' money as you indulged your aesthetic tastes, the limiting factor being the amount of time you could stick being inverted before your eyeballs popped out.

The current advertisement for Reckitts' Blue, which washed as white as any white plugged on TV nowadays, was an azure sea in which an attractive girl drove a speedboat, its wake a dazzling white. 'Out of the Blue comes the Whitest Wash' proclaimed the hoardings. I could get the same effect on a cloudless day by turning the Hart upside down, and getting the nose so far above the horizon that the white spray of petrol vapour was outlined against the blue of the sky. I would have liked the opportunity to sell the idea to Reckitts' publicity men, but felt that 'any my superior Officer', as my commission had it, might get too inquisitive as to the source of my inspiration, and clamp down on my pleasure.

Formation flying, too, was fun. We started off in pairs, with instructors in each aircraft, the lead aircraft flying straight and level while the second one crept up on it until it was tucked in with its wing tips about ten feet to the side of, and behind, the leader's wing, so that you made a forty-five-degree angle to the line of flight. This position was maintained by continuous adjustments of the throttle and flying controls. It was a continuous process that at first involved great concentration as aircraft, even in air that seems completely free from turbulence, are always on the move, just a foot this way or that. As one became more skilled, one relaxed. In a squadron formation of nine aircraft it's like being in a school of minnows, all the aircraft floating in the velvety air, rising a little, falling a bit, gaining or losing a little on the flight line, dipping a wing here and there. The movement is only a matter of feet, sometimes of inches, but it gives the Squadron a sense of living, of breathing, as it were.

In bumpy weather it's another story – of continuous, and much coarser, use of the controls as the turbulence slams you all in different directions, and the possibility of collision is well to the fore of your mind. The formation opens out to give more manoeuvring space, and it's a very exciting scene looking down a line of aircraft and seeing, one moment, the underside of the wing of the man ahead of you and the next looking down into his cockpit from above. It's hard, it's exhilarating, and it's a necessary part of one's training for war, as aircraft in formation can give each other covering fire, to cover blind spots under the fuselage, wings and tail.

One inevitably has off days. I'd made a mess of an aerobatic half hour, and back on the ground Hamilton was going through it all again.

'Don't forget, Edwards, you fly an aeroplane like a violinist plays his fiddle; you don't beat it like a bass drum. Sawdust doesn't fly, you know.'

'Sawdust, sir?'

'It's a hangover from the days when all aircraft were made of wood, Edwards. If you mishandled a wooden aircraft to the extent that it broke up on you, that's about all you'd be left with – a couple of bags of sawdust.'

I filed the advice away for future reference.

As our experience increased we moved on to night flying, which started with ground instruction on the flare path. With no concrete runways or electric lighting our source of illumination was the goose-neck flare, a metal can holding a gallon of paraffin, from which projected a spout two feet long and an inch and a half in diameter, hence the flare's name. A thick wick ran down the spout, teased out at the top end and dipping into the paraffin reservoir below. When lit it produced a smoky red flame that would burn for hours. The illumination level was negligible, the small flame being used merely as a mark. For the final stages of the landing the Chance floodlight was switched on. This was a massive affair rather like a searchlight, and was driven by a diesel generator that made a fair amount of noise.

An hour before night flying was due to start, about twenty assorted ranks would assemble under the supervision of the OC Night Flying – one of our instructors. There would be half a dozen trainee pilots, a driver for the tractor which drew the floodlight, an engine fitter, an electrician, fire-fighters, and aircrafthands as general dogsbodies. Before dark the OC Night Flying would have visited the Duty Pilot in the Control Tower and checked all the hazards and obstructions on the aerodrome – soft spots in the grass due to recent rain, trenches dug for various reasons, newly laid grass, etc. All these he would have marked with red hurricane lamps before night fell, and would have selected his marshalling point. There he would place the battery-operated electric signpost to which all aircraft wanting to take off would taxi, there to await permission for further movement on the ground. These operations, necessarily carried out in daylight, would be conducted by the ground crews with wary eyes thrown over their shoulders, as the aerodrome would be alive with trainers taking off and landing by the dozen.

The OC Night Flying would plan his flare path on the met officer's estimate of the surface wind direction after dark, then lead us out on to the aerodrome. The focal point of the flare path was the floodlight, and the tractor would stop where he had indicated, after which one of the goose-neck flares would be lit. If its smoke indicated a wind direction different from the met officer's forecast he might relocate the floodlight, after which each of the trainees would be given a lighted flare and directed, by waving of arms and bellowings, to lay flares at hundred-yard intervals directly upwind. Across the top of this flare path two other flares would be laid to form a T, each of them a hundred yards to the side.

The floodlight was tested, and from then on its generator ran all night, the noise of its diesel engine muted when the light was switched off, but rising to a full-throated roar when the enormously powerful light flooded the aerodrome. By this time dusk would have fallen, and the less experienced pupils would make their first take-offs before it became fully dark. After this the events of the night had to be interpreted entirely through the movements and relative positions of red, green and white lights.

All aircraft carry a red light at the port wing tip, a green one on the starboard, and a white one at the tail, their sectors of visibility overlapping slightly, so that the experienced eye could tell, within reasonable limits, in which direction the aircraft was travelling, whether in the air or on the ground. In addition, in the centre of the top wing we carried a white 'recognition' light on which we tapped out our call signs in Morse code, to draw attention to the fact that we were making a request to taxi, take off or land, as the case may be.

Flare path duty had an atmosphere all of its own. The smoking red flares stretched ahead into the darkness of the aerodrome, and from the control point near the floodlight at the bottom of the T the OC Night Flying instructed us in our duties – controlling the aircraft with red, green and white Aldis signalling lamps, with a Very signal pistol to back them up in case of failure. The Very pistol had an enormous one-and-a-half-inch calibre barrel, and could be loaded with red, green or white signal flares. Pointed vertically, it went off with a hell of a bang and the appropriate flare burned its way skywards.

The roar of the floodlight generator drowned out all other sounds, so that the aircraft flew more or less silently, and one watched their green, red and white navigation lights flitting like fireflies on the circuit overhead, controlling them with red and green Aldis lamps. My memories of those spring nights in 1937 were that they were never actually freezing, just pleasantly chilly and stimulating. We dressed for warmth, of course, in greatcoats or Sidcot suits, and wore our flying boots and gauntlets.

When an aircraft was given the OK at the marshalling point it taxied out and lined up on the right of the flare path, its ticking-over propeller a diaphanous circle. When given the green to take off the propeller whirled into invisibility as the throttle was opened, and flames would leap from the exhaust. As the aircraft gained speed the tail would rise and, after a few bounces, the aircraft would sail off into the darkness.

The landings were equally fascinating. The silently approaching red and green navigation lights at the wing tips slowly grew wider and wider apart, and sank lower and lower as the aircraft neared its goal. Then the floodlight would be switched on, and into the light-soaked area the yellow or silver Hart would fly, its spinning propeller reflecting a shimmering image of the floodlight's beam, before slowing into a diaphanous disc as the pilot chopped the throttle and sank to earth. When it was safely down the floodlight was switched off, and the white tail light, twitching left and right as the pilot made rudder corrections, diminished down the winking glow of the flare path.

At intervals we would be sent on lonely expeditions to check on the flares, a half-hour release into a world of your own. Now away from the roar of the generator, you could hear your term-mates' engines as they sailed through the sky above you, and you walked from one smoking flare to the next, checking its paraffin reservoir and keeping a wary eye open in case an aircraft swung and one of your pals made a dirty dart at you.

At times there was more hassle. There were limits to the amount of crosswind a pilot could be expected to cope with at night, so if the wind direction changed to that extent the flare path would have to be realigned, which couldn't be done in much under twenty minutes. No further take-offs would be allowed, and all aircraft on circuit would be brought in before the change was made. Aircraft on cross-country flights returning while the change was in process had to be kept in the air with a red lamp, and there was no means of knowing how much petrol they had left, as we hadn't got radios in those days.

In the dark, the direction of the whole line of flares had to be altered by the OC Night Flying, using his knowledge of the aerodrome when deciding upon which point to pivot the flare path, his decision possibly complicated by any soft patches in the grass due to recent rain. The floodlight might have to be repositioned, the marshalling point too, possibly. We trainee crews took one flare each, changed its position from shouted instructions, and reported back to the new control point as soon as we could. There was relief all round when the flare path was back in operation.

On my first night's duty the OC Night Flying had brought the latest thing with him – a battery-operated portable radio. In the magic isolation of our world around the floodlight we controlled our aircraft against the background of Radio Luxembourg. The Happy Girls and Boys of the Ovaltinies sang to us; Princess Pearl, to romantic background music, advertised a cosmetic that even my wife has forgotten. The agony uncle Your Old Friend Dan gave advice in his usual doleful voice. It was all very sophisticated.

Eventually the time came for our own night flying instruction. We took off about thirty yards to the right of the line of flares, usually did a left-handed circuit and came in to land, judging the approach solely by the angle of the flare path – if the apparent distance between the flares increased you were too high, if it decreased you were too low, the more risky error of the two. In the final stage of the approach the floodlight was switched on, lighting up the whole landing area. After landing you turned and taxied to a marshalling point, where you awaited a green light for permission to take off again. As experience was gained the floodlight was not used at all, and the landing was carried out entirely by the glimmer of the flares, requiring a fair amount of concentration.

A fascinating variation of the night landing was that done using wing tip flares. These were magnesium candles about a foot long, held in brackets under the lower wing. Fired electrically from the cockpit, they gave an intense white light which did not blind the pilot as they were blanketed by the wing. One gauged the final approach to land by the relative angles the goose-necks made with each other and, when near the ground, pressed the flare button in the cockpit. Immediately the earth below was illumined in its brilliant glare. But a disadvantage of the flare was that, once fired, there was no control over it. It had to burn itself out and, on the ground, the tremendous heat could damage the linen fabric of the wing, even set fire to it. After landing one taxied quickly to keep up a good flow of cooling air, but a particularly virile flare could be very harassing, most of all to the cursing fire-fighters who had to dash after the aircraft lugging heavy fire extinguishers across a tussocky aerodrome. The chief use of the flare was as an emergency aid in cross-country flying. If the engine failed it would be a great help in getting you down in a farmer's field.

It was a great thrill, after a couple of hours' dual, to get off solo. As the Hart increased its speed down the flare path you were vaguely aware of ghostly figures standing by some of the flares. Then, after a few final rumbles and bounces, the Hart was airborne. Above the invisible trees the horizon appeared – that faint indication of where the sky ended and the earth began – and you climbed away, brought the throttle back a touch, wound out the radiator and levelled out at six hundred feet, trimming the elevator for level flight.

As you turned across wind you looked for other aircraft on the circuit ahead of you. Ah! There was one, on the downwind leg, his white tail light moving to the left. The light faded, to be replaced by the red one of his port wing tip, which meant that he'd turned at right angles to you, and would soon turn again, for his approach to land. Once on the downwind leg yourself you flashed your aircraft letter in Morse code as a signal that you wanted to land. If you got a green you came in on the approach. If you got a red it meant that there was probably another aircraft ahead of you. I'd been given a red, so where was that other aircraft? The one I'd seen ahead of me was still coming in on his approach, so there must be another one around. Ah, there it was! The green starboard wing tip light of someone coming in from a cross-country, approaching on a right-handed circuit. He must have been given the next green. I throttled back to slow down my progress, retrimmed the elevator, and waited.

The floodlight came on, and I watched the first Hart slide down into its light and land, the light being kept on for the cross-country man, now also on finals, as his red port light was showing. I flashed my recognition light again, and this time got my green from the ground – I'd slowed down enough to give a safe separation between me and the cross-country aircraft. As I turned across wind he landed, and the floodlight was turned off until I was on finals myself.

Then I got a red! I opened the throttle, retrimmed the aircraft and turned out of the line of the flare path. I searched the brightly lit ground below for the reason, but could see nothing. As I climbed to rejoin the circuit pattern the floodlight remained on, an unusual occurrence, and then, approaching the flare path diagonally, I saw a pair of red and green navigation lights flashing intermittently, a distress signal, and a priority demand for a quick landing. As I watched, an Audax slid to earth, landed safely, and taxied straight onto the tarmac. I'd find out later about the emergency; possibly he'd got lost on a cross-country flight and was short of petrol, or had engine trouble of some sort. Anyway, he was safe now. I flashed my aircraft letter again, got a green, the floodlight came on as I approached, and I flew, like a moth, into its brilliant white light and landed. I'd soloed at night! One more step up the ladder.

As one flew round in the darkness further from the aerodrome the only real navigation aid was the street lighting in the towns – Market Drayton and Shrewsbury. Out in the country one watched the headlights of cars travelling on the otherwise invisible roads, and in the hills to the south of Shrewsbury one got a further variation on this. A slight glow on the horizon would indicate a car climbing the far side of a hill. As it reached the summit the headlights flashed brighter and, rural English roads being as twisty and windy as they are, the beam would inevitably swing right or left like a searchlight, often shining directly into one's face before carrying on to fade into a tiny glow before descending.

Later on in the term we used the Audax, not the Hart, for night flying, its twelve-foot exhaust pipe becoming a thing of beauty at night. The first half of the pipe glowed a bright cherry-red, which gave me a fright the first time I looked outboard. This was followed by six feet of pipe closed at the end but perforated with dozens of holes to allow the exhaust to escape sideways. The slipstream had cooled the gases by the time they arrived in this section so that its length was filled with an ethereal, flickering blue light, visible through all the holes. I used to stick my head over the side of the cockpit and, with the cold night air battering away at my face, watch that flickering blue light and feel worlds away from those unfortunate millions out there in the darkness, confined to the surface of the earth.

Inevitably, after a while, I had to abandon my dream world and return to another pleasure, that of guiding this throbbing flying machine through the black velvet night skies.

Chapter 3

The Spreading of the Wings

My first real fright in the air came after practising solo forced landings in an Audax. I'd wound in the radiator to keep the engine warm on the glide, had made a fairly good pass at the field and climbed away over its herd of blasé Friesians to carry out the next exercise. At 1,500 feet a plume of smoke suddenly streamed from under the engine cowling. Not just a wisp, but a solid, evil tube of smoke streaming back along the right side of the cockpit.

FIRE! About the most frightening thing that can happen in the air. 'Action in the event of Fire' had been rammed into all our heads, both in our ground lectures and, even more positively, by our instructors in the air. There was a good incentive to learn and remember it, as the main petrol tank, holding sixty-five gallons, was just the other side of the instrument panel, about a foot from one's knees.

'Fire! Hell, I'm on fire.' Alas, my training went out of the window as fast as I went over the side. Forgetting everything, I ripped off my Sutton harness, reached for the grab handles in the top wing and put one foot on the exhaust pipe, preparing to dive steeply downwards to avoid being struck by the tailplane, which could do anything from cracking a rib to breaking your neck in the powerful slipstream.

'Don't forget to count three before you open your parachute,' said my guardian angel.

'Thanks, mate,' I acknowledged, then took a second look at the smoke. 'Come to think of it, it's white, not grey,' raced my brain. 'More like steam than smoke. Steam! That's what it is, steam. I've boiled the engine.' I'd forgotten to wind the radiator out after my forced landing practise, and the full-throttle climb, with inadequate air flowing through the radiator, had done the trick. 'As pants the Hart for cooling streams when heated in the chase', as *Hymns A and M* have it (and possibly future editions of the *Pilot's Handling Notes for the Hart and Audax Aircraft*). Thoroughly ashamed of my cowardice, I fought my way back into the cockpit against the battering of the slipstream, wound out the radiator, strapped myself in and slunk back to Tern Hill, going through the fire drill again, and very thankful that there'd been no one around to observe the scene.

I was lucky in that I was flying an Audax, and not a Hart. The Hart had no exhaust pipe, so when abandoning we were taught to dive straight overboard. The exhaust pipe of the Audax gave one a better launching platform from which to dive, and the extra second or two involved in getting on to the pipe had given me enough breathing space to assess the true situation. If I'd abandoned that aircraft the most elementary examination of the wreckage would have revealed that there had been no sign of a fire, which would have done me no good at all.

The second fright was far worse. My favourite practice was aerobatics, which were intended to give one confidence, both in the aircraft itself and in one's ability to control it, whatever attitude it was in. One glorious spring day I set off to indulge myself, ensuring before take-off that the straps of my Sutton harness were tight. This harness had an unlocking bolt for use on the ground. You flipped up a latch, and that gave four inches of free play so that you could move your head and shoulders for better visibility when taxiing. Before take-off you relocked it.

I flew out to the aerobatic area, checked that the airspace was clear and went into my routine. As I dived out of a loop I kept the nose down to build up sufficient speed to do a slow roll, pulled up into a climb and started the roll. No sooner had I got on to my back than, with a dreadful feeling of insecurity, I slid out of the cockpit and dropped a few inches earthwards before my shoulders hit hard into the Sutton harness. I had forgotten to relock the harness latch before take-off!

My feet could no longer reach the rudder bar, my left hand was flapping ineffectually in the region of an equally inaccessible throttle, and my parachute pack had slid up behind my rump and was wedging me away from the backrest. My right hand, fortunately, was holding the spade grip of the control column, and was joined by the vice-like grip of my left as I clung on to the only thing capable of giving me a feeling of security. But by clinging on to it with both hands I was ensuring that I could no longer use the only accessible control to right the aircraft. Sooner or later I would have to let go.

The engine, now starved of fuel, coughed and backfired its way into silence, and the propeller windmilled slowly into a diaphanous disc. Messrs Reckitts would have appreciated the white plume of petrol vapour now pouring from the air vent in the wing tank, but the vapour sprayed into my face, stinging, freezing and burning all at the same time, and my next breath was almost entirely petrol vapour, my vocal cords snapping shut in protest as the pungent draught swept into my lungs. If ever a chap needed his mother it was now.

As the nose was now starting to drop below the horizon to initiate a lethal inverted dive to the earth a few thousand feet below, I forced myself to take my left hand off the control column so as to get a grip on the cockpit coaming and allow myself to relax enough to use my right hand again. There were two ways out of the situation: to roll out, but there wasn't the rudder control to make a decent job of it, and to loop out, the only way left to me. As I eased the stick back the Audax swung earthwards at gathering speed, the wind starting to sing in the bracing wires. My vocal cords relaxed enough to expel the petrol fumes from my lungs, only to snap shut again as the next acrid breath seared past them, bringing tears to my eyes. The speed was building up enormously, the slipstream ramming my shoulders against the headrest and my head backwards as far as it would go, increasing the asphyxia. I felt that loss of consciousness couldn't be all that far away, but at last the flow of choking petrol fumes was ceasing, and I took great gulps of fresh air. I still couldn't build up enough G to push me back into the cockpit – I'd have to wait a bit – and meanwhile the ground was getting perilously close. What *was* it that Hamilton had said a week or two before? 'I don't mind what you get up to in the air, Edwards, as long as you don't hit the ground while doing it.'

41

He was going to be bloody annoyed with me this time when they scraped me off the deck.

As we reached the vertical a wood swung into my vision and, as it passed out of sight, a field and stream. At last I was slipping down into my seat again, but the wind was shrieking in the wires and the Audax was vibrating to an alarming degree. Though double-handed back pressure on the stick was now having an effect we were still in a hell of a dive, but petrol was now getting to the engine again and it banged and exploded into life and, with the throttle still open, the revs shot screaming off the clock, the engine howling for mercy.

A biplane in the sort of hurry where it has outrageously exceeded its maximum permitted speed can't be ignored. Held together by bracing wires of different lengths, thicknesses and tensions, the strident chord produced as it flies through the air like a subsonic harp is awe-inspiring and deafening. And talking of harps, there was a distinct possibility that I'd be starting my introductory lesson on one in the near future. The harp effect was reinforced by a brazen snarl as the over-revving propeller tips went supersonic, but at last I was safe, levelling out a nerve-shattering hundred feet above the ground, to take my howling, snarling, vibrating machine at an unheard-of speed towards a herd of Friesians, peacefully grazing their way to the next pinta a few fields ahead. We must have seemed like the Angel of Death to them, in each bovine mind the peaceful image of the milking parlour being replaced by a vision of the abattoir. They scattered as chaff before the wind, were lost to sight, and I swept upwards to safety, snapping the harness latch into place with shaking fingers.

Such an experience is, alas, only the penultimate one: there remains the unpleasant business of getting your nerve back, and I gave myself plenty of height for this, climbing to 5,000 feet. With a mile of airspace beneath me for recovery I double-checked my safety harness, dived to pick up some speed, checked that safety harness yet again and initiated the roll. She went round like a bird, so I did one more for luck. With 4,800 feet still in hand, to *prove* that I hadn't lost my nerve, I spun off the next 3,000 of them in the whirligig of a six-turn spin.

Behind one of the large 'C' type hangars was a graveyard of elderly cars, abandoned by our predecessors as being beyond reasonable repair, and they were there for the taking. To teenagers of the economic underclasses logbooks, road tax and insurance were figments of the imagination of the administrative classes. I also saved a further five shillings as I hadn't got a driving licence, having taught myself to drive by watching my uncle, Mad Dick, and borrowing his Studebaker one day when he wasn't looking. (Before you condemn us too much for irresponsibility you must remember that there was little traffic on the roads in the thirties, and the chances of an accident were negligible in the country.)

Gibson, another ex-schoolboy entrant, and I did a tour of the graveyard when we considered that we were financially stable enough to run an untaxed and uninsured car, our eventual choice being a handsome, open-top Alvis 12/50 racer, which had the advantage that it was so long since it had been taxed that its tax disc was nearly the same colour as that for the current year. It had the fiercest clutch of any car that I have ever driven, and lacked any form of self-starting system, even a winding handle, so that it had to be push-started. It had a lighting system, but lacked a battery, so that we always had to get home before dark, or formate on co-operative term-mates, preferably two, with us in the middle. We rarely exceeded sixty miles an hour in it, as even ignoring noises of distress by things like big end bearings and tappets, the bonnet used to fly off at this speed, and we were nearly decapitated the first time it happened. We became quite used to this as, however strong the string we used to tie the bonnet down, it eventually wore through. As soon as the lid started the wild hammering which foretold its imminent flight we ducked beneath the dashboard until the final screech of metal, followed by a darkening of the sky, gave us the information that we could now raise our heads in safety again, stop, and recover the equipment.

We sped up and down the Shropshire lanes in it, extending our knowledge of the Shrewsbury bars, and were all set for the happiest of impecunious summers until, as we swept over a hump back bridge which crossed a stream, a puppy ran out and vanished with a thud beneath the car. I stopped, feeling very sorry for the puppy, then even sorrier for myself, as the village bobby was leaning against a wall twenty yards away, smoking his pipe. I sat unhappily in the Alvis, for with no tax, insurance or driving licence, I visualised that the hideousness of the court action to follow would inevitably lead to a demand that I resign my commission as being a disgrace to the Service. I'd seen a film a year or two before where Captain Dreyfus, an unfortunate French cavalry chap, had had to stand in front of the paraded regiment and have all his brass buttons and insignia cut off by the adjutant before being dismissed in disgrace from the parade ground. Fortunately, they hadn't extended the treatment to his trouser buttons.

I wondered, in my misery, if Mr Roberts was still holding open that ghastly vacancy in his chartered accountant's office. Gibson wasn't looking any too happy, either. By contrast, the village bobby seemed very comfortable, continuing to lean against the wall, and as a scuffle beneath the car led to the reappearance of the puppy, apparently none the worse for wear, he took his pipe from his mouth, said 'Dog's all right, zur' and replaced the pipe. The incident, as far as he was concerned, was closed. But we had a stalled engine and a tax disc as off colour as I was. I hissed to Gibson, 'Get out of the car and stand in front of the tax disc,' and asked the policeman if he'd kindly give us a hand to push-start the car. The cop took a cliff hanging thirty seconds to consider the proposition before removing his pipe for the second time and agreeing, and another thirty seconds to knock it out. Then he gave the car such a shove that it started immediately. The unprepared Gibson had to grab the back of the hood and scrabble his way over the petrol tank into the back seat before he could rejoin me in the front. We waved our thanks to the policeman, took the old 12/50 straight back to the graveyard and left it there. It had been a timely warning.

Guest nights were held once a month, social occasions when one could invite friends for dinner. They were also part of our training in how to conduct ourselves as officers and gentlemen, both categories behaving oddly at times. Togged up in mess dress, with its bum-freezer jacket and its narrow overall trousers strapped tightly under our patent leather wellingtons, we worked through the formal dinner. After that the port circulated, and woe betide the pleb whom the Mess President detected short-circuiting the system by passing it to a needy friend on his right. The loyal toast was then drunk, after which smoking was allowed, and the evening became a free-for-all, the basic requirements being those of hard drinking, horseplay and the singing of dirty songs.

I intensely disliked much of the horseplay, for which we took off our jackets and undid the straps of our mess overalls so as to give more freedom of movement. Rugby scrums were supportable if you liked them, but I loathed High Cockalorum, in which a few people leaned forward against a wall, supporting themselves with their palms. A member of the pack would run forward, jump in the air and land on top of their backs, followed by more and more until the whole pile collapsed in one dreadful heap of, perhaps, twenty bodies. My minor claustrophobia was as nothing compared with my terror of suffocation. In my panic I was gifted with the strength of ten men as I fought my way upwards to freedom.

While young enough to enjoy my new-found freedom of alcoholic excess, and the permissiveness of being allowed to bellow out the dirty songs, it was becoming obvious that the dirty song was on its way out. Few officers, even the more senior, remembered all the words, so that many of them petered out halfway through. But though the old ways were undoubtedly being abandoned as childish, they were an unconscionable time a-dying, even in a service as yet only eighteen years old, and a highly technical one at that. But intelligence was slowly being applied to traditions, our motivation being to be better in the air than any other flying service, and to be worthy of our forebears of the 1914–18 war. We were luckier than the Navy, who had Nelson's long-dead boot on the backs of their necks. But the diehards fought a determined rearguard action, the dirty songs coming up time and time again, though still to peter out after noticeably decreasing intervals, despite the best efforts of sycophantic and red-faced aficionados.

Some of the songs were quite funny, others not so, but all were tried. The sexual exploits of Eskimo Nell were lauded to the skies. The Cruise of the Good Ship *Venus*, whose 'figurehead was a whore in bed, the mast a rampant penis', included in its verses the occasion when 'The captain's second daughter/Fell into the water./Delighted squeals reveal that eels/Have found her sexual quarter.' And there was the versatile Salome, who could '*Run, jump, fight, f...,/ Wheel a barrow, drive a truck.*' But over the years they were sung less and less, and intelligence and ingenuity became the hallmarks of RAF hell-raising. On the credit side, I suppose the self-discipline imposed by not letting on about the more disagreeable aspects of horseplay was to have its uses in the difficult years that lay ahead.

While I spared no sympathy for the passing of those aspects of the old days there was one aspect of traditionalism that, had it been put to a secret ballot, I would have voted to double, and that was the amount of time devoted to drilling on the barrack square. Lined up, with rifles on our shoulders, we would be marched up and down the parade ground by a drill sergeant. We formed fours, moved to the right in columns of fours, presented arms, wheeled left and right, stamped our feet and, above all, swung our arms. 'Swing those arms, gentlemen. SWING them. SWANK!' he would roar. To one such as I, who lacked forcefulness in his personality, drilling was a wonderful release. To be allowed to swagger, swing one's arms and stamp one's feet was very pleasant indeed. To be *made* to do so was sheer bliss. I enjoyed every minute of it.

But audible criticisms of rifle drill as an aid to flying arose on all sides.

'What the hell's this caper got to do with flying a Hart?' muttered McCall, ever the rebel.

'Yes, damn nonsense,' I mendaciously agreed. Whatever else happened, I did not want to become a marked man.

The only hazard of rifle drill was in fixing bayonets, as we weren't allowed to look down at the rifles as we clipped them into place. The whole thing had to be done by touch, and inevitably some did not latch home. At the next 'Shoulder Arms' they flew upwards, to arc down in lethal flight. In the rear ranks one kept a good lookout for them.

'Today,' said Hamilton, 'we are going to perform "Restarting a Stopped Airscrew".' (As we had no self-starting systems in our aircraft it would be a serious matter if our only engine stopped in flight.) 'Take her up to 6,000 feet.'

I climbed through a scattered four-tenths of cloud at 3,000 feet and got to height.

'I've got her,' said Hamilton as he took over the controls. 'Now we've got to stop the engine, which will take some time as the slipstream will keep the airscrew windmilling. I've throttled back, switched off the magnetos and I'm holding her just above the stall.'

We slowed, and with the nose well above the horizon, wallowed and slithered about, but the airscrew still windmilled, so he side-slipped the Hart, skidded into a flat turn, side-slipped again and cried 'She's stopping.' With a jolt the airscrew jerked to a halt, its hitherto half-visible disc converting to the yellow piece of linen-covered wood that was our sole means of propulsion. I hoped that this trick was going to work.

'Now we've had to stop the engine artificially, so switch on the magnetos again.'

'Done, sir.'

'Right. Now in the reality the reaction must be immediate. We don't ponce around losing height.'

He rammed the Hart into a near-vertical dive, and I was grateful when my stomach left my thorax and returned to its more usual location in the abdomen. As the speed built up the slipstream screamed through the wires, and the Hart went into its heavenly harp routine, the sound level building up as fast as the altimeter needle was winding down. Mother earth seemed to be getting too close for comfort as I stared at it over the nose and past that damned useless wooden airscrew. I had the feeling that we were on a loser.

'Sir,' I shouted down the Gosport tubes.

'Speak up, man, I can't hear you.'

'Sir,' I bellowed, 'just to the left of the air intakes you'll see quite a good field – the one with a pond in it. If we pulled out now I think I could get her down in it successfully.'

I hoped that he could detect the note of pleading in my voice.

'Wait for it, Edwards, wait for it,' roared Hamilton. 'You've got to react the moment the airscrew starts.'

'*If* it starts,' I muttered. Too loudly.

'I heard that, Edwards. Don't be so bloody bolshie.'

The noise and vibration were approaching the level when I'd fallen out of the cockpit during that infamous slow roll, the one that I couldn't tell Hamilton about, and I was leaning to the opinion that maybe Bolshevism had a lot going for it when a ray of hope appeared. The airscrew blade moved a fraction to the right.

But it stopped.

Again it eased over, though obviously with the greatest reluctance, flicking through half a revolution before the twenty-one litres of dead engine stopped it in its tracks with a thud that shook the already suffering airframe. Then, again resisting all the way, the blade got on the move, stopped, moved yet again and then vanished into invisibility as the engine fired, the revs shooting up way into the red, despite the closed throttle. Hamilton pulled all the G in the world and we shot straight up to 3,000 feet with no effort at all.

'Now, don't forget, Edwards. This exercise is to be carried out only under dual instruction.'

As he spoke the engine died, and his voice came down the tubes again. 'Okay, that field you were rabbiting on about on the way down. Your engine's failed. Get me down in it.'

'Are there any mushrooms in it, sir?'

'We'll find out when we get there.'

As I flew contentedly home Hamilton interrupted my reverie.

'Edwards, if you ever *do* have a solo crack at that restarting caper for God's sake remember to switch on your magnetos again.'

'Yessir.'

I did. But halfway down the dive, with the spires of Shrewsbury centred between the air intakes on the nose, I was still regretting my decision.

As the Junior Term drew to a close we sat our examinations in ground subjects and completed our basic flying training. As I passed the watchtower on one of those leisurely, end-of-term days a group of instructors was leaving the Chief Flying Instructor's office, Hamilton among them. He'd been newly promoted to Flight Lieutenant, so I went over to congratulate him.

'Thank you, Edwards, but I'm not the only one to be congratulated. We've just finished the Chief Flying Instructor's meeting. I've got your flying assessment here.'

God! I thought of the time I'd nearly baled out after the 'fire'; of the unlatched slow roll; of the forbidden restarting of my stopped airscrew. Maybe I *had* been seen after all. But Hamilton was smiling.

'Yes, take a look at it.'

He handed me my Flying Logbook. I stared unbelievingly at the two statements in it: 'Proficiency as pilot on type – Exceptional.' (The highest there was.) 'Any special faults in flying which must be watched – None.'

'Congratulations, Edwards. You're my first.'

'Thank *you*, sir, for all your help and understanding.'

There remained a further pleasure – the Wings Passing-Out Parade, which involved half an hour of my beloved arms drill in front of the Air Officer Commanding, after which he presented us with the coveted pilots' wings, to be sewn on to our tunics for all the world to see. As I had accepted the inevitable, and bought a second uniform for my 'Best Blues', which had plunged me even deeper into debt with Gieves, I had got my batman to sew a spare set of wings on to my other tunic, in readiness to wear in the mess that night. Along with other clued-up members of the Junior Term I was now indistinguishable from those of the Senior Term, who would soon be leaving for their squadrons.

We went on a fortnight's leave, by which time my family were better educated in matters pertaining to the Royal Air Force, apart from the inevitable aunt who still asked if I was allowed to touch the controls. I caught up with my family, and with news of the outside world, that had seemed of lesser importance compared with the world of flying. The Spanish Civil War continued to rage, a complicated war in which the ideologies of the combatants had got mixed up with those of Fascism and Communism. Once the Russians became involved it gave Hitler public justification for backing Franco, and a wonderful opportunity for trying out the weapons that he was going to use in the war to come, especially the Messerschmitt 109 fighter which was to bedevil our lives in 1940.

Of the blockade-running ships of the nations favouring one side or the other, that of the Welsh sea captain 'Potato' Jones was probably the most famous. For days Potato Jones played a cat and mouse game with hostile naval and air patrols, but eventually got his welcome load of potatoes into one of the blockaded ports, where the inhabitants had been nearly starved into surrender. My family's only *personal* involvement in Spanish affairs was our collie dog, Alfonso, who had been named after the deposed Spanish king.

CHAPTER 4

THE NEST IS FLOWN

On return from leave we were now in the Senior Term, to do our applied flying in the Audax, the dual-controlled Harts being used only occasionally for spot checks on our flying. The Audax carried full military equipment of guns, bombs and camera, and we pupils were now paired off to fly alternately as pilot in the front seat, or in the back cockpit to do gunnery, bomb aiming and camera exercises. I was paired with a New Zealander called Lucas.

Luke, an elderly twenty-three from my eighteen-year-old viewpoint, had come off a sheep farm, and was a rough-hewn country lad who at first had been bewildered by, and slightly contemptuous of, the sophistications of British society. But already he was softening up as a result of his experiences in the last six months. He no longer sounded off about the sissiness of our wearing brown leather gloves, even in the height of summer, and wore, without complaint, the mandatory hat which we all had to wear when in civvies. Unable to buy an outback style of hat in our decadent country he had settled for one like mine, an over-large trilby selected by my mother after seeing George Raft playing a tough part as a Chicago gangster. I didn't like my hat, and later on, when I could afford a fashionable pork pie replacement in an attractive shade of green, I blew my hat up during a mess party on Guy Fawkes' night. A Ha'penny Demon firework had enough power, when it exploded, to blow the hat ceiling-high, and for some obscure aerodynamic reason it spun rapidly as it did so. Such a hilarious performance had to be repeated, and the unwanted hat was soon reduced to shreds, being followed by those of other enthusiasts who could afford the luxury. The multiple launches were the most fun, and the subject of many a side bet. But Luke hung on to his trilby, which quite suited his rough-hewn features.

He and I developed quite a camaraderie as we worked at our routines in the air. With fewer instructors to keep tabs on us we had more freedom of action, and it was an accepted perk of the Senior Term that we could shoot lines to the local girls, who often watched the flying by sitting on the fence of the main road which ran alongside the aerodrome. We made our landing approaches as low as we dared without arousing the wrath of our instructors, so as to make the girls jump off the fence in real, or affected, terror. From the back cockpit we blew them kisses, or made gallant comments, though sometimes ungallant ones. I had succeeded in producing a flurry of summer frocks, bare legs and knickers as the girls got off the fence in a hurry when Luke, leaning as far out of the back cockpit as he dared, shouted 'What hairy legs' at one up-ended girl. I felt that that was going too far.

During those weeks in 1937 when Luke and I were working up, the papers and wireless seemed full of aviation news. On 3 May the enormous German airship *Hindenburg* took off from Frankfurt to cross the North Atlantic. A luxury airliner, *Hindenburg* boasted single cabins for those who wanted them, and even had a grand piano to back up the dozens of crates of champagne aboard. Three days later, when landing at Lakehurst, New Jersey, she was destroyed by fire, and thirty-three people died. The other German commercial airship, the *Graf Zeppelin*, was immediately withdrawn from the South Atlantic run as a result.

We had already abandoned these huge lighter-than-air machines, whose chronic weakness was the highly explosive hydrogen gas which they used as a lifting medium. In 1930 a government-built airship, the R101, had given incessant trouble, and was seriously short of lifting capacity. Despite this, the then Air Minister decided to fly out to India in her. Doubts were expressed all round about the airship's capability of doing this, but they were brushed aside, and the minister even had his official red carpet weighing 1,000 lbs put on aboard. The grossly overladen airship finally ran into high ground near Beauvais in northern France, and was destroyed in the inevitable hydrogen fire. All the passengers died, and only six of the crew survived. And now *Hindenburg*'s destruction would spell the end of German development of these impressive, but lethal, aircraft. In any case they were doomed, as the commercial airliner was becoming capable of longer and longer flights, and at much higher speeds. As a demonstration of this, three days after the *Hindenburg* disaster two Americans, Merrill and Lambie, flew press photographs of the crash non-stop across the Atlantic, landing at Croydon. Three days later they flew back to the States, this being Merrill's fourth transatlantic flight that year.

On 12 May we all had a holiday for the Coronation of King George VI and Queen Elizabeth and, a fortnight later, I was allowed to fly the hottest aeroplane in the RAF – the superb single-seater Hawker Fury, the first service fighter to exceed 200 mph. It was a delightful aircraft, and those of us destined for twin-engined squadrons (as I was) were allowed one flight in it as a special treat, and under pain of unimaginable punishments if we bent it. It went like hell and handled like a feather. A couple of days after my trip in the Fury Britain took the world altitude record, when Flight Lieutenant Adam took the Bristol 138 monoplane up to 54,000 feet.

Amelia Earhart, the American airwoman who'd flown the Atlantic and many other long-distance flights, went missing over the Pacific while attempting a round-the-world flight with a Captain Noonan. On 2 July they left Lae, New Guinea, for Howland Island in the Pacific, but didn't arrive. For several days after, radio signals were received to the effect that the plane was still floating, but none of them gave their position, and they were never found. At the time it was accepted as just another casualty in the expansion of aerial flight, but since then many exotic theories have been propounded as to what lay behind it, among them that the CIA was involved, that the second pilot was a drunk, and that they had been sent to photograph Japanese military installations.

The next day, 3 July, Imperial Airways inaugurated a new air mail service to Durban in the 'C' class flying boat *Centurion*, carrying a half-ounce letter for a penny ha'penny. Shortly afterwards a modified 'C' class boat, the *Maia*, got airborne in the Medway with a 'piggy-back' aircraft on its back. The Short-Mayo Composite Aircraft, as it was called, was designed to release the smaller craft so as to carry 1,000 lb of mail non-stop for 3,500 miles. Later it was hoped to develop it so that it would fly non-stop the 6,000 miles to South Africa. A further Imperial Airways project, jointly with Pan-American, was going well too – double flights across the Atlantic of the *Caledonia* and *Clipper III* flying boats having now taken place for the second time. Day by day the world was getting smaller, and day by day the RAF was getting bigger. New aerodromes were being built all over England and, as far as we could gather, all over Germany too.

As the Senior Term progressed, Armament became the main subject. The Audax had a fixed Vickers machine-gun firing forward, the whole aircraft having to be aimed at the target, and it was necessarily synchronised so that the bullets would not hit the propeller blades. On a revolving mounting in the rear cockpit was a Lewis gun, for which we carried five drums of ammunition. Bombing practice was done with small eleven-and-a-half-pound practice bombs, which gave a visible cloud of smoke on impact.

Both our guns gave trouble in the air, as their rates of fire had been speeded up from those of the infantry weapons from which they were developed, and they just weren't up to it. It wasn't too difficult coping with a jammed gun in the rear cockpit as the gunner could use both hands, but the pilot needed at least one hand to fly the aircraft, and a jammed Vickers in the front was a nuisance. In view of its unreliability, the breech of the gun had to be in the cockpit, so that the pilot could get at it to clear the stoppages, fiddling and hitting and cursing at it as he broke his fingernails and strove to fly at the same time. Fortunately, we didn't have to go to war with this gun as it was replaced by the Browning, a virtually stoppage-free weapon. The reliability of the Browning removed any necessity to have the gun breeches accessible to the pilot, and wing-mounted guns, which had the added advantage that they didn't need synchronising gears, became standard in single-engined aircraft. All this was, however, in the future; we were stuck with what we'd got.

For the last month of the Senior Term we flew to Sutton Bridge, an Armament Practice Camp on the Wash in Lincolnshire. Here we fired live ammunition, and dropped practice bombs, together with the occasional 'Flying Pig', 112 lb high-explosive bombs left over from the 1914–18 war. An odd design, they were nearly as wide as they were long, and it wasn't unknown for them to tumble end over end in their downward flight, hence their name.

Joscelyn du Boulay, an instructor, flew the Audax for my first practice in firing the Lewis gun from the back cockpit. We were flying at about a hundred feet past the line of targets on the ground when several hundred sparrows got up in front of us. With no chance of avoiding them they, or their corpses, hurtled back through the flailing airscrew and scattered themselves over the aircraft. Unfortunately, one had vanished down a carburettor air intake, the Kestrel engine registering immediate disapproval. One smashed the windscreen, several hit me remarkably hard blows on the head and body and one particularly unobliging specimen ended up in the ejection port of my Lewis gun. Blood and feathers were strewn the lengths of the flying wires and several holes in the linen fabric of the wings started to enlarge as the slipstream tore at the flapping edges. I removed my gauntlets and gouged ineffectively at the sparrow-pulp blocking the Lewis.

'Don't bother, Edwards' came down the Gosport tubes, 'I'm taking this heap home.'

With the engine running roughly, as we were now running on one-and-a-half carburettors, the pilot jacked his seat fully up so that he could see over the top of the shattered windscreen and we flew back to Sutton Bridge and landed.

'Well, Edwards,' said du Boulay as I waited deferentially for the debriefing, for the words of wisdom that would stand me in good stead for the rest of my flying life, 'that's two dozen sparrows that will never fornicate and fly again, what?'

An occasional hazard was the 'runaway gun', when the synchronising gear jammed, in which case the front gun just wouldn't stop firing. As the bullets went in the direction in which the aircraft was pointed the pilot had to continue out to sea, so that they fell within the safety area. This went on until he ran out of ammunition or could persuade the gun to stop firing, risking dislocating his thumb as he tussled with a cocking lever that was flogging backwards and forwards fifteen times a second. A more serious aspect, though, was that as the synchronisation was inoperative the bullets could now hit the revolving propeller blades, at best upsetting their balance so that the engine vibrated and, in the extreme, shooting one of the blades right off, in which case the enormous imbalance could shake the engine out of its mounting.

On the second Lewis gun exercise Lucas and I were teamed up as usual, Luke flying the Audax from the front cockpit. I was firing at ground targets and getting fed up with the fleetingness of the target. We could only fire over the side of the back cockpit in the space between the wing and the tailplane and, even at our relatively low speed of 120 miles an hour, there wasn't much time to get off a good burst. Racking my brains for a method of speeding up the process it occurred to me that there was a small 'empty' rectangle between the flying wires running up to the top wing and the side of the fuselage. As long as the shots were kept within that area the aircraft wouldn't be damaged. As the sights of the Lewis gun were four inches above the barrel it could be fired with impunity in the upper part of the rectangle, because when the sight line touched the wires the bullets would still be four inches below them. The converse, however, would require a more delicate approach: I would have to stop firing about six inches *before* the sights bore on the lower wing. A dummy run without firing seemed to indicate that the system would work.

I got off three shots between the wings on the next run, then immediately swung the gun mounting backwards so as to fire over the side in the orthodox manner. It worked like a charm, but I thought I'd better not let Luke know what was happening in case he was of nervous disposition. He'd be far happier remaining ignorant of what was afoot. Unfortunately, on the next run I had to change the angle of the gun, and the empty cases being ejected after my magnificent seven-shot burst flew forwards into his cockpit. As the glinting brass cases hit the instrument panel and tinkled down into the bowels of the Audax, Luke came to life.

'What the hell was that?' he shouted, then looked sideways and saw the barrel of the Lewis pointing incriminatingly between the wings. His voice rose an octave and doubled in volume.

'You aren't shooting *between* the wings, are you?'

'Just the odd round or two, Luke. Not to worry.'

'Are you crazy?' he yelled. 'You'll shoot the effing wings off her.'

The impossible happened. His voice rose a further, incredulous octave.

'My God, you *have* shot the effing wings off her, you sonofabitch. Look at that lower mainplane.'

I looked. There were seven holes in it. I'd fired seven shots! But I wasn't *that* bad a marksman.

'Look, Luke, I can't have fired through the wing unless the barrel's bent, which it isn't. There's something funny up.'

'Funny peculiar, not funny ha-ha,' said Luke sarcastically. 'Anyway, I'm off home before that wing falls off.'

'It isn't *going* to fall off, those holes are in non-vital areas. And you can't go home before I've fired my detail or they'll be down on me like a ton of bricks.'

'Make that two tons,' said Luke hard-heartedly, 'have one on me. I don't know what plans *you've* got, but *I'm* off home for a new set of wings.'

'Oh no you're bloody not. What about that fishing boat?'

'What fishing boat?'

'You know damn well what fishing boat – the one you bombed last week.'

There was a few seconds' silence.

'Oh, *that* fishing boat.'

A few days earlier, with me flying and Luke in the rear cockpit, he'd mistaken a fishing boat for the target, and dropped a bomb on it. He missed by a mile, and the bomb fell so far away from both boat and bombing range that nobody saw it. I'd covered for him by reporting that the bomb hadn't exploded.

'Luke, I'll swap you one unexploded bomb for seven innocuous holes in a mainplane and, if you're nervous, bring the speed back to a hundred.'

Luke agreed. I fired off the rest of my ammunition, Luke made a gentlest-possible landing, and we got hold of an armourer.

'Shooting *between* the wings, were you, sir?'

'Yes, corporal,' I admitted shamefacedly.

'Ah, well, it's not too bad. Take a look at the undersurface.'

There were no holes in it!

'It's the wads. There's a cardboard wad between the cordite and the bullet in the cartridge case and these get blown out of the muzzle after the bullet. The slipstream has blown them backwards into the wing. A rigger will fix it for you.'

The Sergeant Rigger was a kindly soul, not inclined to report me to my instructor.

'If I were you, sir, I'd slip half a crown to Corporal Jackson. He'll put patches on the wing now with red dope, let it dry over the lunch hour then put a coat of silver on them, ready for the afternoon's flying. No one will be any the wiser. Just taxi her over to No.2 Bessoneau.' (Sutton Bridge still had these wood and canvas hangars left over from the Great War.)

As we walked over to the mess for lunch Luke broke the silence.

'Shooting between the effing wings,' he marvelled.

'Bombing bloody fishing boats,' I countered. 'What on *earth* would our mothers think?'

Pipes were now all the rage among the Senior Term and, although I didn't smoke cigarettes, I made a noble effort to go with the trend, buying a briar and an ounce of tobacco. Unfortunately, smoking made me violently ill, not just a little nausea here and there but a humdinger of a vomiting reflex which left me in a cold sweat, and weak at the knees.

Lacking the moral courage to defy my peers and kick the habit, I was reduced to practising in my room, armed with the full box of matches necessary to keep a pipe going for more than ten minutes, and a bottle of lemonade. As the nausea approached I laid off smoking and swigged some lemonade, which quelled the symptoms enough to carry on for another few minutes until the next wave reduced me to prostration. Within a fortnight I could cope with the first third of the pipeful, and found that this was quite enough for me to maintain my position in society. Lighting up with the rest of them I toyed idly with the nauseating object, and talked at such length that nobody noticed that I wasn't actually *smoking* the pipe. Before the end of the term, however, I became my own man, and flung the pipe away.

The weeks at Sutton Bridge had been interesting, but the flight back to Tern Hill was memorable. At 120 miles an hour the twenty-four assorted Audaxes and Furys flew as two squadrons of twelve aircraft. With Luke in the gunner's cockpit, I was in the second squadron, half a mile behind the leaders, but as we approached Tern Hill we seemed to be catching them up. (At the acrimonious post-mortem afterwards it transpired that the leader wanted us to appear over Tern Hill as one impressive formation, so he'd throttled back to a hundred to allow us to close the gap.) Unfortunately, the leader of my formation wasn't prepared for this, and it looked as though we were going to fly right into them. As it became obvious what was going to happen the leading aircraft went to full throttle to try and get away from us and we, in the second squadron, throttled back to avoid hitting them. The result was that when we did finally fly into them we were all going at about the same speed.

The twenty-four aircraft got into a formidable tangle right over the aerodrome, for all to see. (A similar cock-up had happened about 2,000 years before, when a chap called Horatius was guarding a bridge somewhere, those behind crying 'Forward', while those in front cried 'Back'.) As our squadron slid into the leader's, each aircraft exploded into action as its pilot saw an opening to safety and went for it. I started a diving turn to starboard to avoid chewing the tail off the Audax ahead of me, and as my wing lifted over his rudder the landing wheels and long, stalky undercarriage legs of a Fury slid the length of my upper wing, far too close for comfort. As my dive continued another machine below me was itself lifting up from another potential collision, both pilot and gunner looking steadily away from me at their own danger spot. I heaved back on everything, half expecting a tearing impact as my wheels tore into his centre-section. It didn't happen, but it left me in a well established climbing turn, to find the sky above me filled with a yellow-painted aircraft climbing similarly but, alas, not so fast.

'What on earth's a Hart Trainer doing in the middle of a bunch of dogfighting Audaxes?' flashed through my mind, and I hoped that it wasn't some unfortunate member of the Junior Term who had suddenly found himself in bad company. The way we were heading his airscrew would take me in the cockpit area and, whatever lay below me, it could not be worse than the vision of that flailing propeller about to make a pulp of my head, so I shoved the stick forward and went, something making me look over my right shoulder, and I'd have been happier not doing so. Filling my vision, an Audax was diving down on me, the pilot invisible in the shadow of the top wing, but the look of horror on the gunner's face was the only thing needed to initiate my instinctive reaction to prevent him from hitting me amidships – hard back on the stick and full right rudder, knowing in some nagging way that there was something inherently wrong in the action.

It clicked! I was all set up for a flick roll, a manoeuvre that the Audax would take at a reasonable speed, say a hundred miles an hour, but not at the hundred and fifty I'd achieved in the dive. She was going to shed all four wings as soon as the flick developed. Scared stiff, I reversed all controls, but I had already got over the vertical, and came round to be carried back into the whirling dance of death, finding myself formating on an Audax on a very similar course, a refreshing change from the divergent attitudes of the last bunch of aircraft.

Halfway through congratulating myself that we were, at last, out of the wood, I saw his rudder go full over to the left as he saw some hazard ahead, and he skidded flatly across my nose. I lifted my wing tip over his tail and swung away into clear air. Clear, that is, until a Fury in a hell of a hurry swept right across my nose. By the length of pilot sticking out of its tiny cockpit like an asparagus stalk I knew it was the six-foot-four-inch Jim Nicolson, in three years' time to earn the only Victoria Cross awarded to a fighter pilot in the Battle of Britain as he struggled in the cockpit of his burning Hurricane, and, five years after that, to vanish as one of the many 'Missing, believed killed' in the wastes of south-east Asia. I hit Nic's slipstream with a thud, and then we were out in the clear.

'You know, sir,' said my batman as he laid my mess kit out that night, 'that was the most magnificent display of flying I've ever seen, just like the dogfights of the Great War. It was Ball and McCudden all over again. All we batmen think that your term are the best fliers who've ever been through Tern Hill: we really do, sir.'

I didn't disillusion him that he'd nearly witnessed the biggest flying accident in the history of the Royal Air Force.

'Well, we do our best, Keeling.'

The Armament Practice Camp had been the culmination of

our training. There followed the usual delight of the Passing-Out Parade, with the band playing as we marched and counter-marched, fixing and unfixing our bayonets, forming fours and moving to the left in columns of fours, and advancing to our front. We swung our arms and swung them again and swanked, just as our drill sergeants had told us. I wouldn't have swapped places with any other eighteen-year-old in the world.

And so we finally marched off the parade ground, fully fledged Acting Pilot Officers, and no longer On Probation. We were on our divergent ways to join our squadrons, in my case No.233 General Reconnaissance Squadron of Coastal Command, whose motto was 'Fortis et Fidelis' – Strong and Faithful. I hoped to be both.

CHAPTER 5

MONOPLANES, FOR GOD'S SAKE!

M ost people took a fortnight's leave before joining their squadrons, but I didn't want to wait, and got on a train to 233 Squadron's station at Thornaby, in Yorkshire.

Both the mess and the living quarters were wooden huts of 1914–18 vintage, and a pretty drab collection they were. The partitions between the rooms were yellow-painted strawboard about an inch thick, insufficient to prevent sounds from passing through. Each room had an iron bedstead, a table, chair, easy chair, coal scuttle and bookcase, but the room was so small that the bookcase had to be put on the table. In one corner was a coal-burning stove, its cast-iron flue backed on two sides by asbestos sheets as a fire precaution. The window was small, so the room was dark. The ablutions – loos and baths – were similarly divided by strawboard partitions, but these ended a foot from the bare concrete floor, so that draughts of cold air blew unceasingly throughout the lower layers, rarely falling below six on the Beaufort Scale – that at which 'Smacks shorten sail'. In winter, however hot the bath, one's feet usually froze by the time one got back to the fug of one's room. The remaining furnishing of each room, the chamberpot, was just the right size for draining oil from the sumps of the cars of those well-heeled enough to own one, though some wags grew bulbs in them.

The aircraft, too, were a disappointment. The Anson was a hastily modified small civil airliner designed for economical operation, a poor foundation for a military aircraft. It was underpowered, and by the time they'd put two machine-guns and the rest of the military equipment into it, the weight of bombs that it would carry was a disappointing 280 lb. It was, however, a technological advance, being a monoplane, but this was viewed with a certain amount of suspicion. Having been trained on biplanes held together by a collection of wires which you could *see*, we weren't all that enthusiastic on being faced with a single wing with no visible means of support, and we were reinforced in our doubts by the fact that aerobatics were forbidden on the Anson. The wing was of wooden construction, and creaked and groaned when taxiing on rough ground, or in bumpy weather in the air. It was, however, a remarkably efficient machine for its power, had a retractable undercarriage (though this had to be wound up and down by hand) and possessed what was probably the biggest advance in flight safety yet – the new six-instrument blind-flying panel with its artificial horizon and gyro direction indicator. That was worth a lot.

Just as our Anson was the product of the rapid expansion programme so were the personnel. We had only two experienced officers, our Commanding Officer, Squadron Leader Wallis, and Flight Lieutenant 'Monty' Banks, who commanded 'A' Flight. The remaining pilots, both officers and sergeants, had all left their flying training schools within the last two months. Similarly, in the ground crew technical grades a few experienced NCOs were in charge of the newly qualified tradesmen who serviced our aircraft. We were a band of 150 vastly inexperienced men, and were fortunate in having two years in which to get ready for our war. When it did arrive, in September 1939, we were a reasonably effective outfit, apart from our woefully inadequate Ansons.

The new-fangled retractable undercarriage caused some bother at first, as people kept forgetting to wind it down for the landing, which resulted in the two airscrews being bent into shapes that would have inspired Salvador Dali. It also shock-loaded the crankshafts. This expensive pastime was countered by mounting a Klaxon horn a foot from the pilot's left ear, and this went into unmistakable action if the throttles were closed when the wheels were still up. A disadvantage was that in a steep descent, when the throttles would be closed, the horn nearly drove one demented, so a modification to the system was introduced by some pilots which consisted of reaching up in fury and ripping off the electrical leads, the descent then being continued in perfect peace. After landing the pilot told the electrician to reconnect it. Or he should have.

Inevitably, sometimes he didn't, and some other pilot would come in a few days later and bend another couple of propellers. It got to the stage where the CO announced a fine of five pounds for the offence, the money to be paid into the Squadron charity fund. Mike Clarke and Terry McComb, who had taken a fortnight's leave from Tern Hill before joining the Squadron, were taken in hand by Squadron Leader Wallis personally for their conversion course. One sunny day, those of us who weren't flying were lying out on the grass watching the CO give Mike and Terry landing instruction and, as the wheels were still up, it was obvious that he was showing them what *not* to do. Alas, he came lower and lower and slower and slower until the propellers hit the ground and the Anson sank on its belly and slid a hundred yards before stopping. Our hoots of laughter were rapidly stifled as the CO stepped out of the machine, and we all streaked away to find profitable occupation as far from his office as possible. To give the CO his due he did, after an hour's simmering in his office and giving the unfortunate adjutant hell, hand over a five-pound note for the Squadron fund.

No. 224 Squadron, only about a month older in experience, or lack of it, shared the station with us. From scratch, both squadrons had to train in their role of maritime reconnaissance, which meant endless lectures in navigation given by the Station Navigation Officer, another old hand, and followed up with increasingly complex navigation flights, at first over land but later, almost exclusively, over the sea. Our wireless sets rarely worked, as our wireless operators were pretty green, and far less experienced, relatively, than we were as pilots, and this led to a great deal of strain in bad weather, when the radio bearings so essential to our safety were frequently not forthcoming.

It took its toll. In the next eighteen months we had three fatal crashes, the first to go, unfortunately, being Monty Banks, our only Flight Lieutenant, who vanished into the sea one night somewhere near the Outer Dowsing light vessel. And Lowden, our Cranwell-trained adjutant, crashed in the Cleveland Hills to the south of us. Thirteen people died in these crashes and it left the CO with no officer above the rank of Pilot Officer. Dai Davies was appointed adjutant after Lowden's death and I was surprised at his cheerful acceptance of his fate of flying a desk. But with the maturity of his twenty-three years he appreciated the insight which the job gave into the organisation and administration of the RAF. Grass hopper-like, I continued to revel merely in flying.

Lowden's death introduced us to a custom of the service that seemed, at first sight, heartless – that of auctioning off the deceased's kit to his brother officers. The thinking behind it was that the parents of the officer might be well off and would have no use for many of the service items, whereas many junior officers were struggling, and could do with cheap ways of making up their kit. With the next of kin's permission, the auction would take place in the mess anteroom and would start with the CO's statement that high bids were not essential, an indication that the parents did not need the money, or a hint to the contrary, in which case the bidding would be high. I bought a few of Lowden's things as I wasn't all that well equipped myself.

At the sales of dead aircraftmen's kit the prices were almost always high, as the likelihood was that the widow or parents would need the money. It was quite touching to see an Aircraftman 2nd Class, the lowest paid man in the service, bid twice its new price for an oil-stained tunic that he couldn't wear without first paying for it to be dry-cleaned, unless he relished a rollicking from his disciplinary Flight Sergeant. Frequently, after bidding, the item would be tossed back for re-sale. It was an indescribable aspect of service life that would never obtain in Civvie Street. Only within our closed community could the full appreciation of such actions be accepted as the norm, and be expected when the situation arose.

Thornaby was on the edge of the Teesside industrial area, and it was unfortunate that there was virtually no official social contact between the two communities: we had to find our own fun. On a Saturday morning's bus outing to Darlington my Flight Commander, Pilot Officer 'Inde' Cooper, stopped at an antique dealer's shop window. He pointed to something.

'Damn nearly as old as the Vickers guns we've got in our Ansons, aren't they?' he said.

I followed his gaze, and my pulse rate went up. In an opened mahogany case lay a pair of flintlock duelling pistols, complete with their powder flask, bullet mould and cleaning rod.

'Come on, chaps, let's have a look,' I said.

We swarmed in, and the dealer got the case out of the window.

'How much?'

'Four pounds.' A minor fortune!

'What's the least you would take?'

'As you're so young, we'll make it three pounds ten.'

'You're not thinking of buying them, are you?' said Cooper.

'No. I *am* buying them.'

'At three pounds ten! That's half a week's pay. Have you *got* three pounds ten?'

'Er, no, I was hoping I could borrow some. I've got a quid and enough for my bus fare home. Can you chaps lend me two pounds ten between you?'

An air of reluctance was manifest, but they coughed up, and I became the proud owner of a first-rate pair of flintlock duelling pistols.

A visit to the station blacksmith produced a bullet-casting kit of scrap lead, a pair of tongs and a small melting pot, and with the coal stove in my room stoked up to red heat, the lead started to melt. The bullet mould was dirty, so I gave it a good wash, which turned out to be a bad idea. Some years earlier James Watt had discovered the 'expansive power of moisture rarefied by heat', and thus invented the steam engine. I re-discovered it as soon as the molten lead was poured into the wet mould for the first bullet. At about a hundred times faster than it had poured in, the lead came out again with an explosive crack as the water turned to steam, showering me and the room with hot particles.

After that it was plain sailing, as the mould was now dry, and I cast a couple of dozen bullets. All was now ready for the initial firing tests, at first with a blank charge. I primed the pan with powder, brought the hammer up to half cock and locked on the safety catch. Pouring the smallest powder charge that the flask would throw down the barrel, I rammed some newspaper on top of it, took off the safety catch and pressed the trigger. The priming powder in the pan fizzed, and a fraction of a second later the main charge went off with a mighty bang. I was surprised at the heavy recoil that a blank charge could produce, and became aware of an object snaking away rapidly into the middle distance. I had forgotten to remove the ramrod! But the gun had stood up well to the abuse, and I retrieved the ramrod some two hundred yards out on the aerodrome after a search.

The hut I lived in contained twenty rooms, ten either side of the corridor, but only seven of them were occupied, all on one side. The other residents of the hut were becoming quite interested in the pistols, and suggested a penetration test. After loading, with a bullet this time, we all went to the end room of the unoccupied side of the hut, where I pointed the pistol to the middle of the asbestos sheet behind the stove and pressed the trigger. Indoors, the noise of discharge was formidable, and the room filled with the customary smoke of a black powder discharge. We went from room to room, tracing the bullet's path through the holes in the asbestos, and were pleased to find that it had gone through seven of them. It left, of course, seven rooms with inter-connecting spy holes, but the chances of anyone having to occupy those rooms was negligible; even our two squadrons couldn't fill the place. Subsequent firing tests showed the pistols to be extremely accurate, but their main use was to be with blank charges only, a double load of powder with newspaper rammed down on it as a wad. They made an enormous bang, gave off clouds of smoke, and became a useful adjunct to the wilder mess parties.

At about this time a new world air speed record was set in a most exciting fashion. Hitherto, all high-speed flying had been done by the highly specialised Schneider trophy seaplanes, the Supermarine S6B eventually winning the trophy outright for Great Britain in 1931 at an average speed of 340 miles an hour. Two weeks later, with its Rolls-Royce engine boosted to a phenomenal 2,600 horsepower, Flight Lieutenant Stainforth became the first man to exceed 400 miles an hour when he took another S6B to 407 mph, to gain the world speed record for Great Britain yet again. These highly specialised machines were extremely difficult to fly, and required a high degree of courage from their pilots, but the experience gained with these racing seaplanes was to have an important influence on the design of that historic aeroplane, the Spitfire. But now, six and a half years after Stainforth's record, an absolutely standard RAF landplane was to achieve a similar performance. On the night of 10 February 1938 Squadron Leader Gillan took off in the then hush-hush Hurricane fighter from Turnhouse aerodrome, near Edinburgh, climbed up to 17,000 feet and flew south to Northolt at an average speed of 408 mph. True, he made full use of a northerly tail wind, but it was still a hell of a performance, and brought the landplane speed record also to Britain.

With the large industrial complex of Teesside pouring out smoke and pollution the visibility in the Thornaby area was frequently bad, accompanied by unpleasant smells dished out by the huge ICI factory at Billingham. When flying northwards anything up to a hundred miles out to sea we knew when we were off the Tees, as the visibility would steadily deteriorate, and the smells would frequently be detectable.

In February 1938 'Hoppy' Hopkins, who was captain of the aircraft, and I had flown a safe distance from the land, dropped an aluminium marker into the sea, and had each fired a hundred rounds at it with the fixed Vickers gun. We were doing more and more machine-gun practice as time went on, and on this particular day I'd fired first, then Hoppy took over for his session before flying the aircraft back. As we went further up the Tees estuary the visibility deteriorated to the extent that, even if we'd seen the Middlesbrough transporter bridge in the murk, we wouldn't have had time to avoid it. Hoppy turned south, and we found some slight improvement, though not enough for comfort, so he decided to force-land if a big enough field turned up – and it needed to be fairly large for an Anson as it ran a bit further along the ground than most aircraft. Surprisingly, one turned up, and Hoppy put it down very nicely.

As is customary, people sprang out of the ground from nowhere, and it rapidly became a social occasion.

'D'you know, this is the first aeroplane that's landed in this field since 1919,' said an old codger. 'Yes, you're the first for nineteen years,' which rather shook me as I'd imagined that we'd have been the first ever. 'Yes, you've landed at the old aerodrome at Marske. Used to be fighters here in the Great War. Camels they were. Now *there's* an aeroplane for you!'

He looked disparagingly at our modern monoplane.

Hoppy and I rapidly reduced our line-shooting to a level acceptable to such a critical audience, and asked to be directed to the nearest telephone. Successfully ignoring the suggestion of a middle-aged man that we could use his, we elected for the obviously more convenient one offered by two girls in their late teens. Having reassured our flight commander that we weren't six feet under, and would come home when things improved, we ended up swigging cups of tea and, I think, mightily impressing the daughters of the house with our accounts of the excitements and perils of Air Force life. By the time we'd eaten the lunch prepared by our hostess the weather had cleared up enough for us to go home. The girls came to see us off, of course, and I rather wished they hadn't as, Hoppy being captain, he sat in state in the cockpit putting on his daredevil act while I slaved my guts out at the winding handles to get the engines started, a most undignified process, especially after all the good work I'd put in over lunch about the more godlike aspects of a pilot's life.

With continued flying practice, the pilots and wireless operators of 233 Squadron were increasing their skills, and bad-weather flying became noticeably less hazardous. The rank of the Squadron commander was upgraded and Wing Commander Croke took over.

Louis George le Blount Croke was impressive. About six and a half feet high, big-built, with a large hooked nose dominating his red face, he was ex-Navy and gave the impression that he had trained in sail. His voice, at full throttle, could be heard above the noise of a force nine gale, his whispers a hundred yards away. He arrived with several good ideas, the best being that, as the Navy that he had been raised in did a Spring Cruise each year, a maritime reconnaissance squadron should do the same. He got clearance from on high and organised a four-day trip that would take us from Thornaby as far north as Skerryvore off the west coast of Scotland, and as far south as Manston, in Kent, taking in the North Sea and Channel light vessels en route. The twelve Ansons were to be fully self-contained apart from fuel and oil, which would be obtained from the aerodromes at which we landed.

It involved a great deal of organisation, as Louis had to persuade Station Commanders to accept an influx of twelve aircraft for refuelling, and to feed and accommodate the forty-eight crew members. As the cruise held only semi-official status an awkward Station Commander could have spoiled things for us, but fortunately everyone co-operated. A nicety of the planning was that we had to have fitters, riggers and electricians to service the aircraft and there was only one place in each machine for such people, the two pilots and the wireless operator taking three of the four available places. By choosing sergeant pilots of the necessary basic trades, enough vacancies were created for Louis to expand the idea and to carry an air gunner in each aircraft, and we were to drop sea markers and carry out machine-gun practice on them when out to sea.

In a speech in Vienna on 27 March 1938 Goering told the people of Austria that their economic life would be amalgamated with that of Germany, and that the Austrian schilling would be abolished in favour of the Reichsmark. He went on, very ominously:

> I must address a serious warning to the city of Vienna, which can no more be called a German [sic] city because there are 300,000 Jews ... We do not want the Jews, neither in the cultural nor economic sphere. But their elimination ... must be carried out systematically. I instruct the Reichsstathalter of Austria to take with all care and within the law, but without clemency, those measures which are necessary for the elimination of the Jews from business and for the Aryanisation of trade and business.

Chilling and merciless words. And only a small measure of what was to come.

The day after that dreadful speech we got airborne on the Spring Cruise, twelve Ansons laden to the gills with spares, engine covers and screw pickets, the latter being necessary as we couldn't be accommodated in hangars at the stations we were to visit. Screw pickets were yard-long spirals of half-inch steel rod, pointed at the end. Three of these were screwed into the ground at wing tips and tail, the aircraft being lashed down to them so that they wouldn't be blown over by strong winds.

70

On the first exercise we flew a complicated course with five turning points, but the Squadron coped well and we landed at Abbotsinch, near Glasgow, No. 269 Squadron's aerodrome, to be greeted by envious leg-pulling.

'Just as long as you don't fire a twenty-one-gun salute as you leave,' said one chap. 'Somebody said that those guns of yours are loaded. They aren't, are they?'

'Of course they are. We hope to get in some grouse shooting as we cross the Lanarkshire moors.'

The weather next day was unkind so we had to stay another night at Abbotsinch, which meant a great amount of rearranging, signals flying the length and breadth of the British Isles. But we got away on the thirtieth, carried out our machine-gun exercises at sea and called in at home, Thornaby, for lunch, continuing on to Manston in Kent for the night. The next morning we did a round of the light vessels in the Channel area, coming back to Manston for lunch, and then did a long, four-hour sea leg out to the Haaks lightship off the Dutch coast before finally returning home. It had all been a great success. No aircraft had gone unserviceable, and few problems had been encountered due to Louis's sound preparation. It was an undoubted feather in his cap.

In the mess that night a party developed as 233 relived the Spring Cruise, and 224 Squadron, with whom we shared Thornaby, started to get uppity about it.

'Look, Inde,' I said to my Flight Commander, 'this bunch need putting in their place. I've got just the thing for it.'

'What's that?'

'My duelling pistols.'

'You're crazy, you can't fire guns in the mess. Two-two-four certainly deserve it, but you can't go shooting the sods.'

'Just blank charges, Inde. They make a hell of a bang, with lots of smoke and it'll scare the hell out of them.'

'Good idea.'

It only took five minutes to go to my room, load them up and pocket the powder flask and some newspaper for wadding. As I returned 224 were still at it.

'Bloody stupid, if you ask me, carrying loaded guns on a

71

navigation exercise,' said Monte Burton of 224. 'Say someone pressed the trigger at the wrong moment?'

'Two-three-three *never* press the trigger at the wrong moment,' I said, drawing one of my pistols and firing it at Monte's feet. At the thunderous roar he disappeared in a cloud of smoke and shredded newspaper. A stunned silence descended on the anteroom for a few seconds, until a 224 type yelled 'The bastard's crazy. Get him.'

In self-defence I fired the second pistol, which made them think long enough for me to retire behind the protection of 233 Squadron and reload. Any future 224 aggressiveness was easily reduced by firing in the direction of the would-be hero, and it had got to the stage where you could hardly see across the anteroom for smoke.

'All right, we capitulate,' said 'Dogshooter' Wimperley. 'It was a jolly *good* Spring Cruise. Now, who's going to buy me a pint to wash that bloody powder smoke out of my throat?'

Dogshooter was a keen sporting shot, and had acquired his nickname as a result of an unfortunate accident when he was a guest at an upmarket shoot. Firing at a low-flying pheasant, which he shouldn't have done, even if it *was* behind the line of the guns, he peppered one of the picker-up dogs in the shrubs behind. The dog came howling out of the bushes, more surprised than injured, and exposed Wimperley's shame for all the guns to see. He'd lived it down in the shooting world, but not in the RAF, and he was a bit sensitive about his nickname. But, along with other insensitive members of the mess, I called him Dogshooter. However, it wasn't to be long before I became a victim of the system myself.

Some of 233 had been to the pictures to see Walt Disney's film *Snow White and the Seven Dwarfs*, but I'd been unable to go as I was Orderly Officer. As they returned a group of them came over to me and examined me at length.

'I think you're right,' said Robinson to Derbyshire. 'Just turn your head a little to the left, Edwards.'

'What on earth for?'

'Small thing to ask. Just do it.'

I obliged.

'Yes, spot on! You see, Edwards, Derbyshire here thinks that you look like Dopey, one of the seven dwarfs.'

'Oh, thank you so much, Derbyshire. And the rest of you for the confirmation. Most grateful, I'm sure.'

'Come on, Dopey, it's not so bad. And you do fire off pistols in the mess, you know. They don't come much crazier.'

'That's gratitude for you! Two-two-four in full retreat after half a dozen shots and that's what I get for my pains.'

It rankled. After I finished my Orderly Officer duties that night I loaded the pistols and went to Derbyshire's room.

'You awake, Derbyshire?'

'Just about. Why?'

'Look, do you *really* think I look like Dopey?'

'Yeah. Spitting image.'

I fired the first pistol, the red flame of its discharge lighting up the room as it boomed out.

'My God, you crazy bastard!'

'Do you still think so?'

'Of course . . . I mean NO,' he corrected, too late. The priming of the second pistol was already burning and the process repeated itself. I shut the door on the room and its sulphurous fumes, got into bed, thought better of it, reloaded the pistols and went back.

'Still awake, Derbyshire?'

'Sod off.'

I fired both guns together, and hoped he'd asphyxiate in the fumes.

'For God's sake leave the poor bugger alone,' came Robinson's protest through the strawboard partition. 'Now do be a good chap, Dopey, and get off to bed. And if you come into my room with those pistols you'll get a boot in the crutch.'

It looked as though I was stuck with the name.

A few weeks later came the final stage of our flight training. Several of us were detached to Thorney Island, near Portsmouth, for the four-month Navigation/Reconnaissance Course. During the nine months we'd been in 233 Squadron we'd gained a fair amount of navigational experience, but we were now moving on to a higher plane.

We practised the various types of patrolling patterns and searches; code and cypher systems were mastered. We also learned ship recognition, it being essential to recognise the ships of our potential allies, the French, and our probable enemies, the Germans and Italians. It appeared to be a merely academic matter, but we also learned the ships of the American Navy, hardly to be expected as enemies, or even as friends, as our interests lay so far apart. I was very surprised, then, on one of our navigation exercises, to find three American battleships sailing up the Solent, their lattice-type mainmasts immediately recognisable. I sent a hasty sighting report back to base, in the hope that my course tutor would take note of what a bright spark he had in his class.

The change of venue from industrial Teesside to Sussex was very welcome, though those of us without cars were out on a bit of a limb at Thorney Island, it being a dead end two miles off the Portsmouth–Chichester road, with no bus service as yet. Lowing herds of RAF personnel went in a continuous two-way stream to civilisation and back along the marsh-strewn road. But it was a pleasant place in which to relax. We roamed the coast from Chichester to Portsmouth, and picnicked on the downs, lying out in the sun and watching the butterflies on their erratic flights. Four of us clubbed together and bought a second-hand centre-board dinghy for five pounds, sailing up and down the sheltered waters of Chichester harbour.

As the summer passed we learned that both 233 and 224 Squadrons had moved to Leuchars, on the east coast of Scotland, a popular move from the reports that filtered back to us. In the mounting international tension over Germany's pressure on Czechoslovakia the navigation/reconnaissance course came to an end, and we took the train for the long trip home to our squadrons in Scotland.

CHAPTER 6

PISTOLS AT DUSK

W e arrived from Thorney Island to find both squadrons, 233 and 224, settled in at Leuchars, which was a well established station on the coast about five miles out of St Andrews, in Fife. The mess was a comfortable old single-storey building and the whole place was redolent of RAF history.

For years it had been the Flying Training School for Fleet Air Arm and Army Co-Operation pilots, and there was also an Armament Practice Camp, with bombing and air firing ranges a few miles away on the beach at Tentsmuir. Earlier in the year we had spent the month of March at Leuchars doing our annual bombing and gunnery practice, and I'd found it a fascinating place, as the Flying Training School pilots wore every conceivable uniform of the fighting services, the mess being a very colourful place.

One thing that had fascinated me was the unique aircraft catapult used for training the Fleet Air Arm pilots. The catapults on large ships, and most of the other land-based ones, were steam-powered, but the Leuchars one was cordite-operated and the aircraft was literally shot into the air. Alongside it was a large crane, and this hauled the Osprey or Walrus amphibian up to be attached to a cradle on top of the catapult. When all was ready, with the engine running at full throttle and the catapult trained into wind, the Chief Flying Instructor approached with a large eight-inch shell case filled with ribbon cordite. He loaded this into the breech of the catapult, and after a final check gave the signal to the operator to press the firing switch. As with a shell from a gun, so with the aircraft on its cradle, though more slowly, the cordite being specially adapted for slow burning. The whole contraption shot forward with increasing speed, flinging the aircraft into the air at sixty miles an hour, the powder gases exhausting themselves in a prolonged hiss of blue-black smoke. At sixty miles an hour the aircraft would fly, just about, so should have sailed smoothly into the air. Inevitably, the occasional student got it wrong, and the aircraft would hit the ground and do the most enormous bounce before getting airborne.

Despite fervent pleas I never got a trip off the catapult; it was too time-consuming and expensive for giving joy rides. However, I *did* get a trip in the little Walrus amphibian, also known as the Steam Chicken or Shagbat. As we alighted on the water in the Tay estuary off Dundee I was expecting to sink gently into the water on the V-shaped planing bottom, but the thud when we hit the water shook the aircraft in every rivet and me to the core. The forward view disappeared in a sheet of white spray, which was vaporised still further as it sailed back over the top mainplane and through the still-revolving airscrew. As we sank deeper into the water, the shocks as we hit the waves decreased in violence, but increased in tempo, until we skittered to rest. It was a most impressive performance. It was repeated in reverse on take-off. As we gathered way the sheets of spray increasingly covered the windscreen, then reached the airscrew, to be further atomised. The periods between the thuds again diminished as we gained speed, and ended in one or two astounding bounds into the air, followed by a final, awe-inspiring crash and sheet of spray that gave us such a kick in the pants that we became airborne. After that it flew like an aeroplane again.

The mounting Czechoslovakian crisis teetered on the verge of war, and a week after my return to Leuchars the Squadron flew thirty miles further up the coast to its War Station at Montrose. No. 8 Flying Training School occupied all the hangarage, barrack and messing accommodation on the station, so we picketed our Ansons out in the open, and a disused factory building was found for our accommodation. We were issued with palliasses, and a load of straw was delivered by a local farmer. For hours on end some people stuffed the palliasses full of straw for beds while the rest of us carried on with the urgent business of making a war machine out of the Squadron.

Telephone land lines were laid on, and an Operations Room

of sorts materialised. Field kitchens were also delivered, to make us independent of the mess for our food, which was a retrograde step as stews now formed the main part of the menu. 'What's on today?' someone would enquire. 'No, don't tell me. It's ringmeat again.' Ringmeat was a derogatory term for meat of poor quality, originally applied to the 'mutton clutch' type of meal served in the Middle East, which was likely to contain ears, eyes and arseholes.

Then they said we had to camouflage our aircraft in the modern drab green and brown. This order was greeted with dismay all round, as our silver-doped aircraft had the Squadron crest on the fins in enamel paints: they were very elegant aircraft. We were told to scrape these crests right off so that we could not be identified if we were shot down over enemy territory. The notion of how we could ever get to enemy territory in our short-range Ansons, except by rail, defeated us, and we were delighted to learn that the Montrose main stores could not supply the necessary camouflage dopes. The authorities refused to be beaten, however, and ordered us to do the job in ordinary household water-paints. As there were few people in Scotland with the bad taste to use such drab colours we had to scour the coastal towns from Dundee to Aberdeen to get the loathsome stuff, and our pretty silver Ansons disappeared for ever.

My penchant for the use of the flintlock duelling pistols in various mess parties had leaked out, and the CO had considered that I would be better employed sublimating my urges by making me the Squadron Armament Officer, a job which I thoroughly enjoyed. I was now to be kept extremely busy. The Vickers and Lewis guns were taken out of their boxes, stripped, cleaned and mounted in the aircraft, as were the cameras. My bombs and ammunition started to arrive, and I led a dog's life finding places to dump tons of high explosive in a station not equipped for it. I'd find a likely spot when no one was looking, bring along my three-ton trucks, unload their lethal cargo, cover it with tarpaulins, and beat it as soon as I could. As often as not a wrathful Montrose senior officer would be baying for my blood within the hour, with some such trifling complaint that I had dumped umpteen tons of high explosive within six feet of the main electricity cable supplying the camp.

At intervals it rained, of course, and those romantic cinema films of the World War One fliers on their grass aerodromes, which we'd avidly watched in the past, didn't seem so appealing now. Looking back on the whole affair, although I was prepared to take on Hitler's Luftwaffe I hadn't the foggiest idea of what aircraft they flew, although we were pretty genned up on his Navy. In the end it didn't matter, of course. Neville Chamberlain brought back his piece of paper from Munich and we all went back to Leuchars and hot baths again. One thing lingered, however. Whenever we flew in rain or hail the household distemper would peel off our Ansons and, in a month or two, we had just about the most scabrous-looking aircraft in the RAF, a horrible mixture of brown, green and silver, a really diseased-looking, clapped-out mob.

Louis Croke, as I have implied, was a fearsome, though kindly, Squadron commander, and allowed up to three aircraft to go away on weekend leave, a concession much used, as many of us were very far from home in Scotland. As soon as one booked an aircraft the buzz went round, and applicants clamoured for places. Although four was our normal crew we would squeeze in a fifth at a pinch, and even six if no one was looking, though a lot depended on how much luggage the passengers brought, those with too-large suitcases being unpopular. Dogs had to be of approved placid temperament.

The London aerodromes were very popular, but also the most difficult to get into as the units based at them got fed up with the hordes of aircraft wanting to converge on them at weekends. To get round this I normally carried my own engine covers, screw pickets and chocks with me so as to be independent of local favour. While most aircraft went to a single destination, sometimes one pottered around the country dropping off chaps here and there. The system wasn't the waste of taxpayers' money that it may appear to have been as the flights were treated as navigation exercises, and the logs had to be handed in to the Squadron Navigation Officer for analysis on return. One had to be at one's destination by four p.m. on Friday at the latest, so that the machine could be refuelled and put away before work finished. On Monday morning one turned up after breakfast and flew back home again.

Sealand, near Chester, was my weekend aerodrome as it was

only ten miles from my home in North Wales. My eldest brother worked in Mold, and possessed an elderly and sluggish Austin Ten. I would fly low over his office, my infringements of the low-flying regulations being looked upon tolerantly by the local police, as I was the only pilot for miles around, and my grandfather was chairman of the magistrates. Alerted by the engine noise, my brother would come out into the office courtyard and give me the 'thumbs up', after which I'd fly off to Sealand. By the time I'd refuelled and accommodated the aircraft he would have arrived at the tarmac to collect me, a true door-to-door service.

It's not often that the youngest son can impress a brother four years older than himself but I initiated a routine for my return to Leuchars. After a good bacon-and-egg breakfast I said goodbye to the family, and my brother delivered me to the tarmac at Sealand, where the other weekenders waited with their suitcases.

'Valentine,' I said to my wireless operator after the first weekend, 'lend my brother your Sidcot suit and flying helmet for a few minutes, would you.'

I dressed my brother up as an aviator, and went to the watchtower to see the Duty Pilot.

'I'm not setting straight off for Leuchars, there's magneto trouble in the starboard engine. They're looking at it now but I want to make sure they've fixed it properly. I'll do a quarter-hour local air test first.'

The Duty Pilot looked at my brother who, in his unease, wasn't playing the part of a wireless operator very well.

'Yessss,' he said. 'Had magneto trouble myself down at Abingdon last week. My girlfriend *really* enjoyed it. Have a good time,' he said to my brother.

'Thanks, mate, won't be long.'

I took my brother round the area and flew low over our house, my mother and some of the villagers turning out for the demonstration which, knowing the local topography, could be made quite impressive. By slipping down into the valley a mile from home I could twist and turn about forty feet off the ground, always out of sight, then, at the very last moment, pull back the stick and rise, as though from the very earth itself, with a roar of mighty engines. It was all very good for one's ego.

79

Louis's weekend system worked well until disaster struck when
three aircraft were away again. Donald MacElvie went north to
Evanton, hit bad weather, and was four days getting back. Terry
McComb flew to Aldergrove, in Northern Ireland, and bogged
his machine in soft ground, upon which it rained more than
ever so that the aerodrome was declared unserviceable for a
week, thus imprisoning Terry there. I did even better, or worse,
depending upon which way you look at it. I was to drop off some
of the passengers at Abingdon before coming up to Sealand. The
weather forecast had been adequate for Sealand but problematical
for the Oxford area, so we set off before lunch to make sure of
getting there. As we flew south in deteriorating weather I was
getting uneasy.

'Don't worry,' said Ali Barber, who was navigating, 'I know
Abingdon like the back of my hand. We'll get in okay.'

I was beginning to doubt it as it was now snowing, and the
visibility was becoming negligible. Flying in snow was aesthetically
fascinating, as the myriad white flakes rushed at you at 120 knots
then parted to allow you to slip through in a snow-free tunnel of
your own, but the reduced visibility was unpleasant. As Ali and I
strained our vision forward we had no time to be astounded as,
on a reciprocal course and only ten feet above us, a twin-engined
Oxford hurtled out of the snow and shot over our roof like a
bullet. Our combined slipstreams hit with an enormous bang that
hammered the Anson into a vibrating mass of wood and metal
that nearly shook the fillings out of our teeth. In the front of the
aircraft we had had that split-second's warning of the bang but,
for the passengers with none, it must have been very frightening.
Ali and I saw the funny side and howled with laughter, watched
by a hostile audience. Then, at exactly the same time, the same
thought struck us both, and we stopped laughing.

'You know, Ali, it wasn't all *that* bloody funny when you think
about it. I'm turning back to Sealand. You'll have to catch a train
from Chester.'

'Catch a train!' bawled Ali, the near-miss instantly forgotten.
'And miss what's being laid on for me! I tell you, that girl's got
boobs like jellies on springs. It's no problem. I'll get you there.
Trust Uncle Ali.'

Foolishly, I did.

'It's dead easy,' he continued. 'We'll get over the centre of Oxford first.'

The snow changed to sleet as we flew ever lower to keep clear of the cloudbase. Some of the dreaming spires woke up with a start as we flashed past a few feet above their weathercocks.

'Okay,' said Ali, 'follow that railway line.'

I did a split-arse turn.

'Now, we'll meet a crossroads – yes, here it is. Now, turn right at the garage.'

No garage appeared.

Funny!' said Ali. 'Anyway, don't worry, the transport café will turn up soon.'

It didn't.

'Look, Ali, you don't know your arse from your elbow. Admit it.'

'Admit nothing,' said Ali. 'What d'you think that is?'

He pointed ahead to the aerodrome becoming visible in the murk.

'Abingdon, smack on.'

He spun down the wheels and we landed in a sudden flurry of thick snow which reduced the visibility to fifty yards. From out of nowhere appeared an unusual object for a grass aerodrome, a stake of wood fully two feet high which some clot had knocked into the ground, probably as a survey mark, and forgotten. It flew past under the mainplane, I felt a jolt, and we came to rest.

'Get out, Ali, and have a look round.'

'Jesus,' he said on his return, 'the whole port tailplane's been knocked off.'

Two of the passengers were detailed to get out and carry the wreckage and we taxied in to the tarmac.

'Bang goes my trip to Sealand,' I moaned. 'We couldn't go shares on that pneumatic popsie of yours, could we?'

'Not a chance,' said the heartless fellow. 'Anyway, let's get off to the mess before lunch is off. Follow me, I know the way.'

We put our heads down against the snowstorm and seemed an awful time getting to the mess. In fact we obviously *weren't*

81

getting there so I stopped a passing airman, who successfully redirected us.

'A pint first, after that lot, and then lunch, Ali. You don't seem all that well acquainted with Abingdon!'

'They must have built a new mess since I was last here.'

As we chomped away at lunch Ali spotted a chap called Waterhouse, who'd been at flying training school with him.

'Hi, Closet! Nice to see you again,' called Ali across the table.

'Ali! What are you doing nowadays?'

'Two-three-three Squadron. Coastal Command.'

'Coastal Command? What the hell's that?'

'Oh, *very* funny.'

A ribbing match started up, Ali getting the better of it as he had a very penetrating voice.

'Trouble with you bomber boys is that you've got biplane minds,' roared Ali. (They were still flying the outmoded Hinds.) 'You *think* slowly, like a biplane flies. And, as for navigation, any time you want lessons just give Coastal Command a ring.'

I felt that in view of his dubious instructions towards the end of the flight he was pushing things a bit.

'Anyway,' said Ali, reducing his voice to a mere bellow that could be heard the length of the dining room, 'I always thought that you were at Harwell.'

'I *am*,' said Waterhouse, in the unfortunate silence that just happened to occur at that moment. 'So are you.'

The hush that had fallen on the dining room lasted fully half a second longer, until the two bomber squadrons fell about laughing.

'God, Ali, you *are* a clot,' I muttered, trying my hardest to look as though I had nothing whatever to do with him.

'Any volunteers for transfer to Coastal Command?' called a wag. 'Applications will only be considered from people as thick as two short planks.'

I slunk out of the dining room, went down to Flights and dug out 52 Squadron's servicing Flight Sergeant.

'What d'you think of this lot, Chiefy?' (Flight Sergeants were often called this.)

'Firewood, sir. You'll need a new tailplane.'

'How long's that going to take?'

'I've no idea, sir. We don't fly Ansons in this Group so I'll have to find a Maintenance Unit that stocks Anson spares. When we *do* get it I'll need a day to fit it, and I may have to get hold of a Carpenter Rigger for that; we haven't got one as our Hinds are all-metal. And it's Friday afternoon, sir.'

I left, depressed: it was obviously going to be a long job.

Ali vanished to the arms of his bosomy girlfriend, and the mess became a morgue as the bomber boys scattered to their weekend activities. The only thing left to me were the dissipations of Oxford night life. If they existed, I didn't find them. On Monday morning I rang the Squadron adjutant.

'Dai, I'm stuck at Harwell with a broken tailplane. God knows when I'll be home, but it's going to be a few days at least. Will you break the news to the CO?'

'God almighty! *you* tell him, I'm not. Donald MacElvie's just rung from Evanton saying the weather's clamped down, so he can't fly back yet. We've had a bloody-minded signal from the Aldergrove station commander saying that Terry McComb is to be shot at dawn, and now you come on the line saying that not only have you broken your tailplane, but you've bloody well done it at Harwell. You *do* remember, don't you, that you signalled that you'd landed at Abingdon? No, the ball's in your court, Dopey my old friend. I'm putting you through to Wing Commander Louis George le Blount Croke, and God help you, mate.'

God was unsupportive. While acknowledging that I couldn't fly with half the tailplane knocked off my aircraft Louis *did* hint, before slamming the phone down, that it would be better for my promotion prospects if I got that tailplane fixed in the next few minutes.

The days went past. Ali Barber rang in each morning to the sound of creaking bedsprings. My money ran out. I was bored to hell. As I walked down to Flights on the sixth day, having nothing better to do, a low-loader overtook me, carrying the most beautiful thing I'd seen for weeks – an Anson tailplane. Within the day it had been fitted, and I rang the CO with the good news.

'Right, Edwards, I'll see you tomorrow.'

Which just goes to show how mistaken you can be.

In doubtful weather we got airborne and, within a quarter of an hour, the radio had packed in. Deeper and deeper into the murk we flew, until even Louis's wrath counted for naught.

'Ali, I've had a basinful. As soon as we hit the A1 I'm following it north and landing at Dishforth.'

'Dishforth? I know just where it is. When we get to Boroughbridge I'll let you know.'

'Please don't, Ali. I'll find my own way in.'

We scraped in by the skin of our teeth and I rang Dai Davies again.

'Dai, guess where we are?'

'Not Leuchars, that I know. Louis's going to be quite disappointed, you know. And the weather forecast for the next few days is awful. Do let me put you through to him.'

Before I had time to plead with him there was a click and I was through. My left eardrum nearly shattered as Louis, in full square-rigger form, came on.

'EDWARDSSSSSSS!'

'Sir.'

'Catch the train.'

'Catch the *what*, sir?'

'You heard. I want you in my office by 1130 tomorrow.'

'Yessir.'

But I was speaking to the air. He'd already slammed the phone down. By the time we'd made the miserable train journey home Louis had cooled off a bit, but the bad weather held for the next three days, after which Dai Davies managed to get out of his adjutant's office for a breath of fresh air, and flew me down to Dishforth to collect my machine. Twelve days after leaving Leuchars K8815, with her spanking new tailplane, was back home in the roost. Having had three aircraft and crews away for a total of nineteen days, Louis was a bit more cautious in his future interpretation of weekend weather reports.

An innovation of Louis's that went down well was the Squadron pipe band. He had started it from scratch when we were still at Thornaby, but it was still very much in embryo. Now that we were in Scotland it was in its correct setting, and Louis pulled out all the stops. Known pipers were posted from units in Bomber and

Fighter Commands, Scottish Command of the Army was contacted for advice, and squadron funds of long-disbanded units were raided for our musicians' fund. The stage was reached when only one more piper was needed. He was located at Gosport, and was persuaded to apply for posting to Leuchars.

Such a treasure merited VIP treatment, and I was ordered to fly to Gosport to collect him. Louis watched my engine-starting routine critically. As the port engine fired he appeared to have doubts as to my suitability for the mission. He clambered into the cockpit and shouted, 'Get him inside the aircraft as soon as you land and *don't* let him go. If you do I'll have your guts for garters.'

'Yessir.'

Louis left, and I fired up the starboard engine.

Louis returned to the cockpit.

'Make sure he wears his parachute and knows how to use it.'

'Yessir.'

As I completed the magneto checks and moved away from the tarmac Louis waved me to a halt. Through my open side window, and above the noise of the clattering Cheetah engines, came the final bellowed instruction: 'If he *does* have to bale out, make sure he takes his bagpipes with him.'

Slowly the band took shape and improved. A retired Pipe Major was discovered living down on the estuary, and transport was laid on to bring him in to the camp. Subscriptions were asked for from the officers, and who could resist the melting eyes, or was it that great hook nose and the power of life and death that Louis had over us? We paid up.

As far as I could gather, the bagpipes of a Pipe Major differed from those of ordinary bandsmen in that the bag had to be inflated with whisky fumes, and I think the officers' subscriptions went entirely to support the Pipe Major, who drank, of course, only the most expensive single malts. Eventually the day dawned when the band was considered fit, not only for the Squadron to hear, but for the whole station, and it appeared on the 0830 parade. As we marched off the parade ground the band squealed and groaned its way through the first few bars and then really got going. If ever pipes skirled it was our mob. It was magnificent!

A Celt myself, though from gentler climes, it fired my blood, and even that of the hitherto lukewarm Sassenachs who formed the bulk of the Squadron.

First we marched, and then we strutted, and then we swanked our way off the parade ground as the music got into our blood. Out on to the main road we went, turned right at the Guard Room and swaggered down to Flights. What clot said that marching had nothing to do with flying aeroplanes? It had *everything* to do with it, especially when you did it to a pipe band. At dining-in nights the band appeared, chiefly for piping in the haggis, a type of Scottish ringmeat. After the bandsmen had downed their allocation of whisky they marched round and round the table as we downed our haggis. The magnificent, barbaric noise set the blood alight, such a start to the evening often initiating the wilder kind of RAF party.

Undoubtedly, the most outstanding pre-war party was that when two motor cycles were brought into the mess. The sleeping quarters consisted of a broad central corridor crossed at intervals by lateral corridors serving the bedrooms. One bike did runs up and down the main corridor while the other did chicken runs across it. With the good fortune born of long experience, backed up by the fact that the Lord usually looks after babies and drunks, the bikes rarely collided, though the likelihood of a smash was, of course, the main attraction of the sport. The noise was formidable, and exhaust fumes filled the place. It occurred to me that it might be more exciting if we used a starting pistol, so I went to my quarters for my flintlock duellers and returned to the fray. In the confined space the booming crash of the first pistol stopped everyone in their tracks, enabling me to explain the reorganised starting system. It also added considerably to the smoke.

With the now highly competitive starts people were queueing up for the chicken runs when the anteroom door swung open to reveal, just discernible through the exhaust and gunpowder smoke, the Station Adjutant in his pyjamas. Despite his unimpressive height of four feet, eleven and three quarter inches, Chota White was a formidable character. (Chota is the Urdu for 'small'.) A Great War pilot, and bachelor, he was the oldest living-in officer on the station, and although only a Flight Lieutenant was a man to be reckoned with. His great weakness was a tiresome insistence on placing people under arrest when he was tight. Fortunately, his memory was of short duration when he was in this state, so the arrested officer would leave the room, wait a few seconds, and return through another door, by which time Chota would have forgotten the incident. Tonight Chota was obviously livid at being aroused from his beauty sleep. He took a deep, fume-laden breath and laid into us. The motor bikes were heaved out of the mess and he suddenly spotted the duelling pistols in my hands.

'As for you, Edwards, you're under arrest. Go to your room.'

I left the anteroom, used the statutory pause to reload the pistols, and returned through the door through which Chota had come in earlier. He was still giving the chaps the rough end of his tongue as I crept up behind him and fired the first pistol. As his enpurpled face reappeared through the smoke like an enraged bull elephant he was obviously on the verge of apoplexy. But, far worse, he was sober. Stone cold sober. And shaking with rage.

'I told you that you were under arrest. Go immediately to your room or I'll send you there under escort,' he roared. 'And I'm confiscating those pistols. Hand them over.'

'Well actually, Chota, one of them is still loaded.'

'Well actually, Edwards, fire the damned thing off then.'

I tried to do this as deferentially as possible, but it's difficult introducing subtle nuances into the discharge of a firearm. I pointed it at the floor and pressed the trigger in as respectful a manner as possible. In its completely disrespectful way the gun went off and, as soon as Chota reappeared through the gunsmoke, I handed him the pistols and went to my room.

Next morning I took vows that I'd never again combine alcohol, exhaust fumes and gunsmoke to quite the same extent. The anteroom, as I passed through on the way to breakfast, stank of fumes and was littered with the shredded newspaper wadding of my pistols. I thanked my stars that the Station and Squadron commanders were all married and living out of mess, as they'd cashier the lot of us if they saw the state of that room. At table most people sat like bears with sore heads and fiddled with revolting things like fried eggs, but Chota White sat behind the *Times* in his usual taciturn fashion. As soon as he sighted me he exploded.

'Don't you know you're under arrest?' he bellowed. 'Go back to your room immediately and stay there until I send for you.'

I staggered back to my room. I needed professional advice, so rang for Brittain, my batman. He'd been in the Marines, so would probably know a thing or two about procedures. He came into the room and started an automatic tidy-up.

'Brittain, I'm under arrest!'

'Oh, I'm sorry to hear that, sir. Anything serious?'

I explained.

'Have you got your *King's Regulations*, sir?'

I pointed it out, and he riffled through the pages.

'I think these paragraphs cover your situation, sir. There seem to be three main charges that could be levelled against you: Conduct unbecoming an officer and a gentleman; Disgraceful behaviour in a professional respect; and Conduct prejudicial to the maintenance of good order and discipline.'

'Nothing, Brittain, under "Firing, when under arrest, a pair of flintlock duelling pistols near the earhole of a Station Adjutant on the only night of the year when the latter was sober"?'

'Nothing, sir.'

But they didn't need it: the first three were a catch-all situation. They'd got me.

'What do you advise, Brittain?'

'I always recommend my officers to have a good breakfast in situations like this, sir. I suggest bacon, eggs and mushrooms to start with . . .'

The floor heaved.

'Jesus, Brittain, not in my present state.'

'Then may I suggest a lightly boiled egg, sir.'

'Just the job.'

'And toast and marmalade to follow?'

'Thank you, Brittain. Just the lightly boiled egg, and one slice of thin bread and butter.'

Ten minutes after I'd finished breakfast there was a hammering on the door and Robinson of C Flight barged into the room.

'Prisoner, attennnnnSHUN! Right turn, quick march, left wheel . . .'

'Oh, shut up, Rob. What the hell do you want?'

'Well, some Alka-Seltzer wouldn't go amiss, but I'm your escort: Chota wants to see you immediately. And don't make a bolt for it or I'll be in the shit, too. I'm still half deaf from those bloody pistols of yours.'

'Sorry, Rob.'

When we got to Station Headquarters Rob was dismissed, and I stood to quivering attention before Chota, who continued signing forms and reading letters for a minute or two, a fairly normal softening-up process. At last he looked up, ominously addressing me by my surname.

'I don't need to remind you, Edwards, of the seriousness of your situation. The discharge of firearms in the mess is an act of gross irresponsibility, but more serious is the fact that you disobeyed a reasonable order to consider yourself under arrest. *King's Regulations*, paragraph 1234567 (ii) (6).' He tapped the open volume on his desk. 'That charge merits my referring you to the Station Commander.'

Twelve feet away through the communicating door the Group Captain could be heard stirring. I prayed that he wouldn't come in.

'The annual recommendations for promotion are due in at the end of this month and I must consider whether or not yours should be deferred until you show a greater degree of responsibility.'

'Chota! Sorry. Sir, you wouldn't do a thing like that!'

'I'll do anything I like, you insubordinate puppy, commensurate with the gravity of the offence.'

'Puppy!' 'Commensurate!' 'Gravity!' Chota was on his high horse. The bell on his desk rang, and he went into the Group Captain's office in answer. As the minutes dragged past I hoped that I wasn't featuring in the conversation. Loss of promotion was bad enough, the loss of cash would be even worse.

After a long absence Chota came back, seemingly very preoccupied. He sat down and looked at me as though for the first time that morning.

'What do you want, Dopey?'

'Er, nothing sir. It was you who wanted me.'

'Did I? Oh yes, these pistols.' He picked them up from his desk. 'Look, Dopey, if you ever fire these damned things in my lughole again I'll bury my boot so deep in your arse that it'll take half your precious squadron to pull it out again. Now get off to work.'

I'd got off lightly. I took the pistols and left.

Chota *had* taken the matter no further. In June they remembered that obligation stated on my commission – 'You are therefore carefully and diligently to discharge your Duty as such in the Rank of Acting Pilot Officer or in such Rank as We may from time to time hereafter be pleased to promote or appoint you to.' Sure enough, up it came. My promotion to Flying Officer was promulgated in the *Gazette* and I was now being paid one pound a day. A few months earlier the national wage for railwaymen had been approved at forty-three shillings a week, a claim by the National Union of Railwaymen for a minimum wage of fifty shillings being rejected out of hand, of course.

CHAPTER 7

MORE SAWDUST

We were fortunate in that Group Captain Baker had stayed on as Station Commander of Leuchars after the Flying Training School left and we moved in, as most of the social contacts formed between the station and the local people were retained, a complete contrast with Thornaby, where we had been an island of servicemen set down in an indifferent industrial environment.

Leuchars was one of the best stations in the RAF, the mess being a comfortable old building with new centrally heated sleeping quarters built on, though messing was a bit expensive. 'Messing' was a system whereby the officers (and the sergeants did likewise) paid to improve their living standards. In the services one never starved, a living ration being supplied daily to each man. As this was pretty basic fare, both officers and sergeants elected to pay extra on their mess bills for the purchase of modest luxuries, chiefly in the food line, but also occasionally in the decoration or furnishing of the mess. The standard charge in most officers' messes was three shillings and sixpence a day, about seventeen pence, but at Leuchars we paid three and nine, that extra thru'ppence making a subtle difference in the standard of luxury in the mess. Messing did, of course, make quite a hole in one's pay, representing about a fifth of a junior officer's income.

Social life was developing – we junior officers had, of course, already done our duty in calling on the married officers, a matter impressed upon us during our commissioning course at Uxbridge . . .

'As to visiting cards, gentlemen, they are not to be these damned modern printed affairs; they must be impressed from a plate so that the embossed lettering can be felt with the thumb. In case any of you had thought of doing it on the cheap the plates have already been ordered and they, and the first batch of cards, will be debited to your mess bills. When you run out of cards just send off the plate to the printers for a repeat order.'

He explained in detail the manner of calling upon married officers and their families – the Station Commander first, then the Squadron Commanders, after which you worked your way through the remainder. It all seemed a bit Victorian, but was founded upon the necessity of maintaining social life in services where you could be moved around the country at frequent intervals, and so could lead a lonely life if things weren't organised. As the British Empire extended over half the earth, you could find yourself in an isolated community in one of the numerous overseas commands such as the Mediterranean, the Middle East, Palestine, Trans-Jordan, Iraq, India, Aden, the Far East. From Chichester to China, Invergordon to India, units large and small were scattered around, and social organisation was a necessity.

The passing years have erased from my memory much of the detail, but one called at teatime. If the hostess was in, the handing over of your card entitled you to your cup of tea and a chat, and I got through a fair amount of Earl Grey on this system, never my favourite tea. If the hostess was out we handed over *two* cards, the corner of one being turned down. Why, I haven't the faintest idea, though it could have been Victoriana for 'Sorry to miss you, luv'. Anyway, by now Leuchars was a well-knit community, and it was obviously time we held a mess party to return the hospitality of the local people. At a mess meeting we voted half a day's pay each towards the cost, and the arrangements got into top gear.

First and foremost was that we had to learn Scottish country dancing, a dance instructress visiting the mess and putting us through our paces. This was great fun, especially the whooping and hopping around in such things as the Dashing White Sergeant, the Eightsome Reel and the Gay Gordons, 'gay' being a happy word in those days. Eventually we became proficient enough for the party to be finalised. Flowers were ordered, a dance band laid on and 233's pipe band was to play for the Scottish dancing. Girlfriends and parents were invited, local people volunteering to put them up for a couple of days. Cross-country flights were planned for purposes not too closely investigated, and we were lectured by the CO on looking after wallflowers.

'If I see *one* girl sitting by herself against a wall I'll know where to look for my Orderly Officers over the next month or two,' said Louis.

The great day came. Early in the morning several aircraft took off on their 'navigation' exercises, the mess was polished from top to bottom, the squadrons' silver laid out. Flowers abounded. At varying intervals the aircraft returned from their navigation exercises, taxiing to within twenty yards of the mess. The Anson doors would open, and Sidcot-suited figures clutching suitcases would hurry over to the quarters, some of them with suspiciously long hair. In the quarters themselves bathwater ran by the hundred gallons; batmen were bawled for and bawled out.

'Simcox', came a shout. 'These wellingtons are a bloody disgrace!'

'It's only the right one, sir. I can't do anything with it. It's never been the same since the motor bike ran over it at that party a few weeks ago.'

'Get a move on, you lot,' bellowed the mess secretary out in the corridor. 'You're on parade in the anteroom in five minutes. Out of here, the whole lot of you, within three minutes.'

By 1930 hours a glossy array of well-scrubbed officers accepted a sherry from the kid-gloved hands of the mess waiters.

'Wouldn't mind a pint at this stage,' grumbled Hopkins.

'Well, you can't have it,' snapped Chota White. 'Indulge your plebeian habits later on, if you must, but it's sherry until the guests arrive. This isn't the bloody Naafi, you know.'

'No, sir. I mean yes sir.'

That first party was a great success, many of us bachelors meeting the girls and their families that were to make our time at Leuchars a happy one. I met Jane who was, she informed me, at the Slade. Whatever the Slade was, it must have been a highly sophisticated organisation, as Jane certainly was: she ordered a dry Martini.

'An American drink, isn't it sir?' said the barman with an air of disapproval that such a thing had got north of the border. 'What they call a cocktail, I believe.'

'I think so, McGarry. Er, McGarry, have you any idea what the Slade is?'

'God, Dopey, you are a pleb,' said Guy Robinson alongside me at the bar. 'It's a fancy art school in London.'

'Thanks, Rob. Got any tips on chatting up a popsy in the art world? I want to sound intelligent.'

'Intelligent! You? Well there's that chap Picasso, of course. He's just painted a thing called "Guernica", about the Spanish Civil War. And there's whatsisname with the sergeant major's moustache – Salvador Dali. Talk about oils and watercolours, things like that.'

Within the week I had my feet under the table at Jane's hospitable parents' house, and started an association with the family that was to last more than forty years.

A few weeks later I travelled down to Woodford, near Manchester, to collect a new Anson from Avros, the manufacturers. The aircraft was waiting for me on the tarmac, but hadn't been test-flown yet.

'Won't keep you long,' said Bill Thorne, Avro's chief test pilot. After climbing to about 1,500 feet he appeared to be in serious trouble, as the Anson rolled over on its back, fortunately carrying on to come the right way up again. By this time I'd caught on to the fact that it was deliberate, that it had been a well executed slow roll. Bill followed it with a loop, and then a roll off the top of a loop. Here was one of these new-fangled monoplanes, twin-engined, and with a wooden wing at that, still in one piece after aerobatics!

'Okay, she's all yours,' said Bill after he landed. 'Sign here.'

'Just before I sign, do you do that to all your Ansons, or was it just to mine?' I thought that maybe he had it in for me.

'Oh, I do it to them all; it's a standard part of the test flight.'

I flew back to Leuchars thoughtfully, as there still lingered in the back of my mind the conviction that the only aircraft one should aerobat were single-engined biplanes, which had all those visible bracing wires to hold them together. But here was the manufacturer's test pilot aerobatting not only a twin-engined monoplane, but one with a wooden wing! I carried the story back to the Squadron and got the impression that, to a man, they fully approved the ancients' habit of executing the bearer of ill tidings.

'You say he *rolled* your Anson!' said my Flight Commander. 'What sort of a roll? Not, for God's sake, a flick roll?'

'Well, more like a cheese and onion roll, really.'

'Oh, *very* funny,' said MacElvie, who was quite old, about twenty-six. 'Now, what sort of roll was it?'

'Just a slow roll, Donald.'

'Just a slow roll the gentleman says,' continued MacElvie. 'I can tell you what's going to happen the next time someone flies into a cumulo-nimbus – he's going to end up flying a couple of bags of sawdust.'

There it was again – the wisdom of generations handed down from father to son by word of mouth. Hadn't Hamilton told me the same at Tern Hill after some ham-fisted effort on my part? 'Sawdust doesn't fly, Edwards, sawdust doesn't fly,' he'd said.

The marked man was at a serious disadvantage in the thirties, so I dropped the subject. But I wanted to have a go myself. It was over a year since I'd done any aerobatics so I was pretty rusty. A loop would be easy enough, but the slow roll was a complex manoeuvre requiring good co-ordination of all three flying controls if you were to do it properly. After a well executed slow roll you should be still pointing at the aiming mark you'd selected before you initiated it, usually some cloud feature. Before I tried that I would like a dual refresher. But that would be impossible in present company; I'd have to look elsewhere for a kindred spirit.

It took a couple of months, then Peter, a new boy straight from flying training school, was posted to B Flight. I offered him a deal whereby he was to gen me up on aerobatics in return for the kudos of being one of the first two Squadron pilots to aerobat an Anson.

'What, aerobat this thing!' said Peter. 'A wooden monoplane?'

'You've got to move with the times, Peter. Bill Thorne does it as a routine.'

'Who's he?'

'Only Avro's chief test pilot.'

'Never 'eard of 'im.'

'Well, you have now. Don't be so bloody chicken.'

'All right. But one proviso – we wear our parachute packs. If you pull the wings off her I want to get out quick.'

(In single-seater aircraft the pilot wore his parachute as an integral part of his equipment – it formed his seat cushion. Twin-engined crews wore only the parachute harness, the parachute pack itself being kept in a quick-release rack. When required it was clipped on to hooks on the front of the harness.)

'Done.'

Taking the dual-control machine on the pretext that I was giving Peter instrument-flying instruction, we flew well away from Leuchars and hid behind the biggest cumulus cloud in the area. We clipped the parachute packs to our chests, and I found that although it got in the way, as I had to bend my arms round it to hold the control spectacles, it didn't seem to interfere with my ability to control the aircraft, an incorrect assumption as it turned out.

Peter refreshed me on how to do a slow roll, but I decided to do the easier loop first, dived to pick up 165 knots and hauled firmly back on the spectacles. She rose nicely into the loop, but as we got over the vertical the control column came into hard contact with the bulky parachute pack on my chest, and would come back no further, even when Peter lent a hand with his own controls. We were about thirty degrees inverted when the Anson stalled on its back. We fell off the top of the loop like a ton of bricks, the speed built up alarmingly, and the wooden wing began to creak and groan. God! What was it that Mackenzie had said only the other month, and Hamilton two years before – 'Sawdust doesn't fly.'

We plunged our shuddering way earthwards, to the shrieking of the slipstream, and finally completed a loop that wasn't quite out of the textbooks, with my heart doing about a couple of hundred to the minute. We both drew breath, and as my pulse rate dropped to an acceptable twice-normal I said to Peter, 'That was a lousy idea of yours.'

'Of *mine*! Yours, you mean.'

'No, no, not the loop, the parachutes.'

'Yes, perhaps they were. We'll have to take them off.'

The next couple of loops were a doddle, then Peter spoiled it all.

'Have you taken a look at the gyro horizon?' he asked.

The author's first flight was in this rotary-engined Avro 504K Barnstormer, flying from a farmer's field in South Wales in 1926. It carried his father, his two brothers and himself as well as the pilot – quite a load for its 130 horsepower Clerget engine.

Brooklands Aviation Flying School, Sywell, Northampton, where the author learned to fly in 1936.

A second-hand Hart Trainer after a pupil's attempt at a 'blind' take-off 'under the hood'. The directional gyroscopes that fed information to the blind-flying instruments were air-driven from Venturi tubes that stuck out into the slipstream. In order to get them working, the aircraft had first to do a circuit. The instructor forgot to do this, so the pupil's reactions to the hideously inaccurate information which he was receiving from his instruments had this result.

An entry in his logbook which pleased the author no end.

TOTAL FLYING ALL TYPES	HOURS			
	DUAL		SOLO	
	52·25		47·25	
TYPE OF AIRCRAFT	FLYING DURING LAST MONTH		TOTAL FLYING AT UNIT	
	DUAL	SOLO	DUAL	SOLO
1 HART(T)	2·15	4·45	18·00	18·45
2 AUDAX		2·10		7·25
3 TUTOR			1·40	
4 HART(1)			2·05	2·15

PROFICIENCY AS PILOT ON TYPE. — Exceptional on Hart(T) and Audax.

To be assessed :- EXCEPTIONAL; ABOVE THE AVERAGE; AVERAGE; BELOW THE AVERAGE

Any special faults in flying which must be watched :- none

C.F.I. — Officer Commanding
10.F.T.S. ROYAL AIR FORCE
Date 24.4.37.

CHIEF FLYING INSTRUCTOR
NO. 10 FLYING TRAINING SCHOOL

Trainee pilots, Sywell 1936. Author back row, third from right.

The Hawker Hart light bomber, on to which the author progressed at No.10 Flying Training School, Tern Hill, Shropshire in 1937. Its 525hp Rolls-Royce Kestrel engine gave it a top speed of 184mph, then quite an impressive performance. *(Rev. Bill Hossent)*

The Hawker Fury, the first RAF fighter to exceed 200mph. Pupils destined for fighters trained on these delightful aircraft. As a special treat, possibly because of the flying assessment shown opposite, the author was allowed to fly one. It was the nicest-handling aircraft he ever flew. *(Derry Matson)*

The tipped-up Anson shows a fairly common occurrence in the days before concrete runways. Grass aerodromes could get very boggy in wet weather, so that even after a good landing one could run into a soft patch, with the above result. *(Wing Commander Derry Matson)*

The cordite-fired aircraft catapult at Leuchars, used for training Fleet Air Arm pilots. *(Ian M. Burns, Toronto)*

Hoisting a Fairey 111F on to the catapult – and ready to go.

Loading the cordite charge. The naval rating is sliding the 8-inch naval gun shell case into the breech, supervised by the Wing Commander Flying. *(G. L. Skinner)*

Hawker Nimrod leaving the catapult.

No.18 Blenheim Delivery Flight. Thorney Island to Heliopolis, July–August 1939. These aircraft were the author's first experience of the new generation aircraft with all mod cons such as variable-pitch airscrews, retractable undercarriages and wing flaps, all hydraulically operated. They were also built by 'shadow factories', not by Bristols, the designers. These were built by the Austin Motor Company and, to the surprise of the RAF, the wings did not fall off. Author, 2nd row, third from left.

Vickers Vildebeest torpedo bomber. The author used one as a runabout to collect engine spares for No.18 Blenheim Delivery Flight. In a strong wind they nearly went backwards. Still in use in Malaya in 1941, such antiquated aircraft got a dreadful pounding from the Japanese. *(Squadron Leader Leslie Holland)*

Author's Hudson under attack by a Messerschmitt 109 in the North Sea. 1940.

Mess party early 1940. The sort of party where, later in the evening, it would become necessary for the author to produce his flintlock duelling pistols in order to maintain a semblance of order. 'Hoppy' Hopkins, who wrote the foreword to this book, at the very back. Roy Fuller, in one of his more subdued moments, extreme right.

Lockheed Hudson. We started the war with our underpowered, under-armed Ansons. Fortunately, under the rearmament programme, our purchasing commissions in America came up with this far more effective aircraft. Ultra-modern for the period, they gave us a sporting chance in the Norwegian campaign that was to come.

The author in 1944.

'Not recently,' I said. 'Oh, hell!'

It hadn't taken kindly to being looped, the horizon itself cowering up in the top left corner of the instrument.

'Gosh, Peter, we're nabbed.'

'Yes, it's a fair cop.'

I flew unhappily home. 'D'you think five bob to the instrument repairer would fix things if we get hold of him as soon as we land?' I said to Peter.

'Well, Dopey, it looks a darned expensive instrument to me. Ten bob would be nearer the mark.'

Ten bob! Half a day's pay just for one lousy loop. Plus a couple of good ones, of course. It was beginning to look like an armoured car job, this!

The Rolls-Royce armoured cars of the RAF were one of the major peace-keeping forces in Iraq, backing up on the ground the air action that kept the warring tribesmen from cutting each other's, and our, throats. They also served a secondary purpose as a school of correction for General Duties officers – the pilots – who had failed exams, pranged aircraft, been insubordinate or otherwise blotted their copybooks. A couple of years on armoured cars were usually enough to cause the miscreant to mend his ways. Anyone who had done a term on them was suspected to have boobed at some time in his career.

In the event it didn't cost me a penny, and I never served in armoured cars. The artificial horizon had re-erected itself by the time I came in to land. If only someone had told me that they did this after a few minutes it would have made for much more peace of mind, but I don't suppose they expected people to put twin-engined aircraft on their backs. But there was a big bonus: it had taught me that monoplanes would take as much hammering as biplanes, and gave me confidence in them. I was moving into the modern era. But I also kept looking over my shoulder at times past. The flintlock duelling pistols had whetted my appetite for old guns, and having read several books on the subject I was now becoming reasonably knowledgeable about them. Though I still had a lot to learn, as I was soon to find out.

When I walked into an ironmonger's shop in St Andrews and saw an 1856 pattern Beaumont Adams percussion revolver hanging on a hook I went for it, trying to beat him down from the outrageous thirty shillings he was asking to a more reasonable pound. We seemed to be sticking at twenty-five shillings when he threw in a sweetener, a part-used tin of Smokeless Diamond sporting powder.

'Is smokeless powder all right for this gun?' I asked him. 'I use only black powder in my flintlocks.'

'No problem at all,' said the super salesman.

I took my treasure home, cleaned it, and cast round for a method of firing it. A visit to the armoury produced some .455″ Webley revolver cartridges whose bullets seemed approximately the same calibre, so I broke them down, poured Smokeless Diamond into one of the chambers in what would have been a small amount had it been black powder, and rammed the bullet home. It wouldn't go in, being vastly oversize. It also wouldn't come out, as it was jammed. By dismantling the gun, and judiciously using hammer and file, at last I persuaded the bullet home. Reassembling the gun, I capped the nipple, presented it to the target, pressed the trigger, and immediately wished I hadn't. The grossly overloaded gun went off with a thunderous roar, and recoiled backwards out of my hand, taking a chunk of flesh out of my forefinger as it did. When I recovered I walked the twenty yards back to where it lay on the ground, expecting to find that it had burst. But, a tribute to the workmanship of its Victorian maker, it had survived intact. I had learned a lesson about firing modern smokeless powders in antique firearms, and decided to get rid of the stuff.

On one of my walks some time before I had come across a wasps' nest built into the ground. Through a one-inch hole the creatures skittered busily to and fro. Wasps are, poor things, enemies of society, so I took my tin of Smokeless Diamond, a flask of black powder and a box of matches, poured all the smokeless powder into the nest and laid a train of black powder for a foot back from it. Having seen Errol Flynn, as a pirate captain, blow up a ship in similar fashion, I could remember the rate of burning: a foot would give me time to get away before it all went up. But Errol Flynn must have been using poor-quality powder, as mine burned almost instantaneously. Still on my haunches, I saw the earth a foot away start to crack and open up, and then the explosion and stinging particles of earth hit me in the face. I ended up on

98

my back, astonished, but not blinded. And then multiple red-hot pains developed all over my chest. Mystified, I opened up my shirt to find a dozen half-stunned wasps who had been blown there by the explosion crawling feebly round. As they recovered their senses they reacted in the only way they knew: they drove in their stings. Ripping off my shirt I beat the survivors to death and staggered home, thereafter only to use black powder where it was meant to operate – in the breeches of guns.

'War Games' were now becoming increasingly common. Over the last two years we had worked up to a fair level of skill in our maritime reconnaissance role, increasingly complex navigational and ship-recognition exercises being practised. These came to a realistic culmination in the Navy's Spring Cruise, when all the Coastal Command squadrons, both landplanes and flying boats, reported continually on the ships' movements. The Navy, of course, made it as difficult as possible for us to shadow them, with highly evasive manoeuvres, especially at night, when we were quite blind to a ship's progress. The onset of dawn would initiate yet another intensive sweep of the oceans until they were found again.

Fighter affiliation was also practised, and we did a memorable five-day exercise with No. 41 Squadron, who flew up from Catterick in their beautiful Super Furys, the ultimate development of the biplane fighter. They were immensely proud of them as they were the only squadron so equipped. Camera guns were fitted to all aircraft and, throughout the week, we worked up to increasingly difficult air firing exercises, the photographs and films being analysed on the ground so that the accuracy of the 'shooting' of the fighter pilots and our air gunners could be assessed.

Our air gunners were not full-time, they were tradesmen such as fitters and riggers who had volunteered for flying duty, for which they were paid an extra shilling (five pence) a day. As they didn't get much practice in peacetime this affiliation exercise was invaluable. We pilots got no gunnery practice with our fixed front guns as we weren't fast enough to catch and attack the fighters; our marksmanship could only be practised at the annual armament practice camp, firing live ammunition at towed canvas targets.

Occasionally I got into the turret myself, to see how difficult our gunners' job was, and also to have a few fun shots at those pretty little biplanes as they came curving in to attack us. I soon formed the opinion that the gunner's job was immensely difficult. Had his aircraft flown straight and level he would have a steady platform from which to lay his gun, but the pilot's job is, of course, to take violent evasive action when attacked by a fighter, the main consideration being to give the fighter as difficult a shot as possible. As soon as his aircraft goes into such a sudden turn the gunner's aim is thrown wildly off, and he has a struggle to get back. With the G forces also in action he may find it impossible. But it is still essential to have rearward defence in a heavy aircraft, of course: the fighter pilot's aim must be put off as much as possible by endangering him with return fire.

On the second morning of the exercise there was consternation as one of the Furys overturned on take-off, the pilot being uninjured fortunately, but subject to much censure as he couldn't give an adequate explanation for the accident. It was very sad for 41 Squadron as there were no replacement aircraft; they were the last of their line. In the afternoon a similar accident happened again, and the horrified Squadron commander nearly wept. Again the pilot could give no acceptable reason for it; he'd felt the aircraft decelerate and swing to the left, and the propeller had smashed as the tail rose and the nose dug in. The wings had been strained enough to be irreparable. Another write-off!

Flying was cancelled for the day, but a conference of pilots and servicing personnel produced no explanation. Next day flying resumed with the Furys opening their throttles very slowly on take-off, and all went well. The Squadron commander breathed a sigh of relief, but the next day he did it himself, and nearly committed hara-kiri. But we now had the explanation. Grass aerodromes could get very boggy in wet weather, and to counter this a 'mole drainage' system had been installed at Leuchars six months before. At six-foot intervals over the whole landing area a special tractor had sunk a steel blade two feet into the ground, opening up a three-inch-wide trench into which was poured a stream of gravel. It had proved to be quite effective, and since it had been installed the gravel runs had become invisible under a growth of new grass. The fat doughnut tyres of our Ansons bridged the three-inch drains with ease, but the Furys had tiny, narrow wheels which could sink into the gravel troughs. On the first and third flying days the wind direction had been well across the furrow direction, so didn't affect them. On the second day it had swung so as to blow almost along their length, and the occasional Fury wheel sank in. It had been a heartbreaking experience for 41 Squadron, with three of their twelve graceful aircraft written off. It is also a great shame, in these restoration-conscious days, that no example of that elegant biplane exists. It went out of service at just the wrong time. With the coming of the war they were all junked for their scrap metal.

The sort of black show that could lead to a posting to armoured cars occurred when we were on detachment at Bircham Newton, in Norfolk. A carload of us, including a member of the resident 206 Squadron, had gone down to the beach at Hunstanton. Finding the tide about a mile out we'd driven the car down to the water's edge, where the fact that we hadn't got bathing suits wouldn't matter. After a refreshing swim a plot was laid and the car drove away, leaving the 206 Squadron man starkers on the beach. He made a dash for the car, skilful driving ensuring that he never quite made it. But in our enjoyment of the fun we'd failed to notice that we'd come much nearer the promenade, and we in the car were also starkers, of course.

'You stupid bastards,' panted the flagging streaker, 'let me into the car.'

'No sense of humour, you two-oh-six types, that's your trouble.'

'Sense of humour! There's probably some retired Colonel's wife with her binoculars on me right now.'

'Well, she *is* going to be disappointed, isn't she?' said someone.

'Look, I've got to *live* here; I won't be hundreds of miles away next week like you lot,' he panted. He made one final plea. 'For God's sake let me in or we'll end up in the cells. We're damn nearly in the main street, you stupid sods.'

We *were* too close to civilisation for comfort, so took his advice and drove him back to the waterline, where we all got dressed.

As we passed Sandringham on the way back to Bircham Newton one of the King's pheasants committed suicide, flying out of a hedge and doing an ill-advised wingover into the car radiator. By a majority vote we retained the corpse for later consumption, but either of our afternoon's actions could have seen us on armoured cars had we been detected.

We returned to Leuchars from Bircham Newton to find that an even more effective fighter affiliation exercise was planned for us. As soon as it could be arranged we were to affiliate with a Hurricane squadron. Now this really *was* getting into the modern age, and we all thanked our lucky stars that we were in a service which welcomed technical development and innovation, which did not apply to the other services to the same extent.

The RAF had started life shortly before the Great War as the Royal Flying Corps, its name betraying its Army background. To a certain extent it was commanded by generals who could not fly, and who had as little appreciation of aviation as some of their fellow generals for the problems of the infantryman in that dreadful war. As an example of hidebound Army thinking, in the days of Marlborough and Wellington the infantryman's Brown Bess musket was hideously inaccurate at anything over a hundred yards, so the artillery could set up their guns a few hundred yards from the enemy and fire away in almost perfect safety. By 1900, however, the magazine rifle could pick off a gun's crew at 500 yards with ease, as our artillerymen found to their cost in the Boer War. The obvious solution was to fit an armoured shield on the front of the gun, but the idea was rejected out of hand, as it smacked of cowardice on the part of the unfortunate gunners, who continued to be slaughtered in the best British tradition.

I imagine that the artillery officer who first put forward the idea became a marked man, with negligible chances of promotion. Eventually, of course, shields were fitted.

This mentality continued into the Great War when the parachute came into use, but only for artillery observers in balloons. Towards the end of the war the Germans introduced parachutes for aircraft pilots too, but the Royal Flying Corps were denied them, again on the psychological ground that it would encourage cowardice in the too-easy abandoning of their aircraft. Hundreds of pilots were condemned to burn to death, or to sit in their crippled aircraft during a prolonged descent, before final impact with the earth put them out of their misery. Even discounting the humane angle, it was a highly inefficient decision. It cost a lot of money to train a pilot, far less to build an aeroplane. A live pilot was an investment who would fly another day.

It was a similar situation with the Royal Naval Air Service in the Great War, and the Fleet Air Arm in the Second World War were pretty hidebound, too. The vast majority of their aircraft were obsolete even before the war started in 1939. The biplane Swordfish that the Navy had as main equipment at the war's outbreak was still in use in 1945. The aircrews of the Fleet Air Arm fought a gallant war with damned awful equipment. It was against such a Blimpish background in the Great War that the more progressive Flying Corps officers at last had their way, and the service became independent of the Army as the Royal Air Force, no doubt to hoots of laughter from the other two services, as this happened on 1 April 1918.

But the system paid off. While we in our squadron still had the misfortune to be equipped with an underpowered converted civil aircraft, at least the thinking was there. Within the month we would be affiliating with a 300 mile an hour fighter. Maybe *we'd* get lucky too, and be re-equipped with a more suitable aircraft one day.

CHAPTER 8

REINFORCING THE RAJ

As a hangover from the days of duelling, three topics of conversation were forbidden in military messes, as they were the three subjects about which it was too easy for differences of opinion to get out of hand. They were religion, women and shop.

The iron discipline of the RAF ensured that the former was never brought up, but had relaxed to the extent that there was fierce competition for the only other two subjects that we ever *did* discuss. Regrettably, at the age of nineteen, for me flying still had a bit of an edge over women, though this was fading. The rest of my Flight were men of maturer years and were biased about ninety to ten the other way. I found that I was taking their advice more and more.

By the time the Squadron got back to Leuchars from Bircham Newton Jane was home on vacation from the Slade, where I gathered that she had not been short of entertainment. But in no time at all her parents had whisked her off on holiday, after which she returned straight to London.

'How's that blue-eyed beauty of yours getting on, Dopey?' asked my Flight Commander on a day when bad weather had us all grounded.

'Back at the Slade, 400 miles away.'

'Well I think I can help. Some secret documents have to be collected from Air Ministry. Like to go and get 'em?'

'Thanks, Inde, you're a pal.'

'Now you haven't forgotten that good advice we gave you the other day about seduction suppers, have you?'

'No, Inde. Just the *right* amount of alcohol, enough to loosen up her inhibitions, but not so much that she gets as high as a kite.'

'That's the stuff! B Flight will be expecting results, you know.'

'You'll get 'em.'

I arranged to collect the documents from Air Ministry early on a Friday afternoon, signalled the London aerodromes for accommodation for an Anson for the weekend, and Biggin Hill came up with an affirmative. As soon as it became known that there was a London-bound weekender there was the usual rush of applicants, and I staggered off the ground with my wireless operator and a card-school of four in the back. By skipping lunch at Biggin Hill and dashing straight up to Air Ministry, collecting the documents and hurtling back, I had them safely locked up in the Station Adjutant's office before work for the day finished. Then up to town again, to organise the seduction supper at a dimly lit haunt recommended by one of the Squadron roués. The soft lights and sweet music seemed just about right as I awaited Jane.

When she appeared she looked ravishing. Her dress, which matched her eyes, would have set me back a month's pay, and there didn't seem to be a hell of a lot of material above the waistline, which was promising.

'Now, what would you like to drink?'

I'd genned up on all the modern concoctions like dry Martinis, Gimlets and White Ladies – no country yobbo, me.

'A dry sherry, please.'

Better still. You could order big 'uns.

'Two schooners of Tio Pepe, please.'

The ultra-large glasses were sampled and approved. With a couple of those under her belt she'd be mooing soon.

'If you'd like to choose your menu I'll order a suitable wine,' I said, waving the wine list nonchalantly in the air, and knocking the entire schooner of sherry down the front of her dress with it. Her cleavage awash with the stuff, Jane leapt to her feet, mopped a bit here and there, and disappeared in the direction of the Ladies. She reappeared looking a bit overdressed in her ocelot coat, but had recovered enough to give me a forgiving smile, which was nice of her.

I chose a really good claret to go with the duckling, and then I did it again! Halfway through a riveting account of the variable-pitch airscrews which were fitted to our latest aircraft I sent her glass of red wine to join the drying sherry stain. Her expensive gown was now looking distinctly second-hand and after that, despite her inherent good manners, it was all downhill.

The fantasy of taking her back to her digs while she slipped into something a little more comfortable was as dead as the duck which was congealing on her plate in a sea of red wine. With her ocelot coat held closely around her we returned to her Bloomsbury digs where, it transpired, there had been an unfortunate mix-up in the arrangements for the weekend, and she wasn't free after all. She turned down my offer to pay for the dry cleaning of her gown, which was a relief as the taxi fares and the hideously expensive meal had nearly cleaned me out. I took the tube back to Biggin Hill and spent a lonely weekend reading the papers and playing billiards with the fighter boys.

I returned to Leuchars on Monday and handed over the secret documents to Dai Davies, the Squadron adjutant.

'Signature please, Dai.'

'Have a good weekend in London?' he said as he signed for receipt. 'Jane come up to scratch? Lots of booze, eh?'

'Yes, Dai, *lots* of booze.'

'Coming for lunch?'

As we walked to the mess Dai said, 'We're off to Wittering tomorrow for a week, so get your crew and aircraft sorted out, and make sure your camera guns are synchronised. We're doing fighter affiliation exercises with Twenty-three Squadron. Hurricanes.'

'So it's come off at last!'

'Yes, Louis's been working hard on this one.'

'Don't know about you, but I'm really looking forward to this.'

Louis led us down to Wittering in Squadron formation, the twelve Ansons making a heart-stopping sight as they minnowed up and down in the velvet-smooth air. Our first action after picketing the aircraft down was to have a look at the Hurricanes. They really were something! They'd do over 300 miles an hour, climb at 2,500 feet a minute, had a service ceiling of 33,000 feet and carried *eight* Browning machine-guns, a hitherto unheard-of armament which spat out 160 bullets a second as opposed to our single Vickers, and its fifteen a second. Still fitted with fixed-pitch wooden airscrews, as their variable-pitch ones hadn't arrived, they were still a very potent machine. (And there were rumours of another fighter, called a Spitfire, which was supposed to be even faster, which took some believing. Things were starting to happen in the RAF.)

For a week we shot at each other with camera guns, and it was brought home to us that as the Luftwaffe's Messerschmitt 109 would be of comparable performance, we were in for a rough time if we were ever caught by a modern fighter. With their enormous speed advantage of 130 miles an hour and that devastating armament, we'd be sitting ducks.

Back at Leuchars we went one stage further in updating our training. Hitherto all our bombing practices had been against fixed targets. As one of our roles in the event of a war would be shipping strikes we needed to practise against moving ships. We would now be able to do so, as an armoured speedboat had been delivered to our Marine Section at Newport, on the River Tay. It had a deck that would withstand the eleven-and-a-half-pound smoke bombs which we used for practice. The boat would go out to sea and wait off the Bishop Rock lighthouse, all shipping in the area having been warned that as the RAF were carrying out bombing practice that day they should divert to another track.

For these exercises I was crewed up with Donald MacElvie, a mature twenty-six-year-old. We were of the same seniority, having both been commissioned at Uxbridge in December 1936, and I don't suppose that we ever bothered to sort out who was captain of the aircraft when we flew on such local exercises, the loose assumption being that whoever was flying at that time was captain. We had eight practice bombs in our racks when we set off for the Bishop Rock that April morning, to find the target boat waiting for us. As the chance of hitting such a small target was remote the boat was armoured only on the top, as it was reckoned that the angle of arrival of the bomb would be so steep that it could not get inside the big overhang of the deck. The crew would batten down all hatches and get inside their steel carapace until informed by wireless that bombing practice was over. They then made their way back up the Tay to Newport. As wireless communication was still not all that reliable in 1939 there were back-up smoke signals. If the radio had broken down, as soon as the crew were all snugged down below decks they would light a yellow smoke candle, indicating that they could be bombed.

That day, unfortunately, and unbeknown to us, they'd been having trouble with the carburation of both engines and, as they lay waiting at anchor off the Bishop Rock, the engine fitter was tinkering with things below decks, the rest of the crew lying around dragging at their Woodbines. As we approached, the fitter happened to initiate a diagnostic start-up of both engines, which gave out great belches of smoke, mistaken by Donald, that hawk-eyed Highlander, for the yellow 'Ready to bomb' signal. He informed me of the start of the exercise and turned in on the bombing run. A mile above the speedboat I went into action as bomb aimer, and dropped a real humdinger on our sitting target. It was the MacElvie/Edwards combination at its best and, had it been a high-explosive bomb, he'd have been blown out of the water.

The reaction of the crew was immediate, those on deck deciding not to finish their Woodbines after all. They dived below and slammed down the armoured hatch, yelling to the fitter to tread on it, which he did. The launch set off for the safety of Newport, its defective engines still pouring out the smoke which we knew indicated a willingness to be bombed. As, like an aerial sheepdog, we hounded our twisting and evasive quarry up the Tay – with a bomb here to turn him right, a bomb there to bring him back a little – the smoke died away as the fitter got things in the engine room better organised. It was replaced by a thick trail of unmistakable red smoke, the emergency signal to stop bombing. Alas, our final bomb was already on its way, and he drove straight through its spray as it hit the water. A mile below us the dinky toy launch turned into the Marine Section at Newport at a speed that I would have considered foolhardy had I been its Commanding Officer.

Probably the most valuable trait in aircrew is that of rapid thinking, of the ability to make instant, correct decisions, and I made one then. I remembered that it was Donald MacElvie who was captain of the aircraft, his broad shoulders being far more suitable than mine for carrying the can that was going to come our way when we landed.

Donald left the Squadron shortly afterwards to do a Specialist Navigation Course. He had applied for the course some months earlier, but when the confirmation arrived it coincided with what appeared to be a monumental error in navigation. The exercise in question had involved flying a hundred or so miles out to sea and returning to the Isle of May, in the Firth of Forth. On the return flight the weather deteriorated, and the visibility dropped almost to zero. As no land had appeared after his ETA had expired he was experienced enough to knew that he was flying westward in a wide inlet of water, quite obviously the Firth of Forth, and he was keeping a good lookout for his main hazard, the Forth railway bridge.

Instead he flew low over a man in chest waders and deerstalker hat, who was wielding a fifteen-foot salmon rod in what he later found out to be the Beauly river, which runs into the Moray Firth a hundred miles or more to the north of the Forth. Not the most scintillating piece of navigation! He managed to get down safely at Evanton, only to have the misfortune to find that Squadron Leader Feeny, our second-in-command, was there on official business. Feeny was not impressed with MacElvie's performance, the error in track being of the order of thirty degrees. By popular consent, MacElvie was awarded The Most Highly Derogatory Order Of The Irremovable Finger, and he led a dog's life for the next day or two. However, it had not been his fault. Or rather, he had not been at fault on that particular flight: it had been on the previous one. Mac's story was that a fuse had blown in the undercarriage system, so that the Klaxon had not warned him that his wheels were still retracted, and he'd landed wheels-up. It was unfortunate that at the last moment, and just too late, he'd realised his error and had gunned both engines just before touchdown, so when they suddenly came to rest they did so from near-maximum revs. Such an event shock-loaded the crankshafts severely, and could slightly deform them, though not always to the extent where it was noticeable mechanically. It was discovered later that they could now generate strong electrical fields which could, and did in this case, affect the compass. Donald had been hoist with his own petard. But we'd learned one more thing, of course, though by this time it must be admitted that even the dimmest type was getting used to these new-fangled retractable undercarriages.

Early in 1939 there was exciting news. Middle East Command was being reinforced with the new Blenheim twin-engined bomber. These aircraft were an enormous technical advance on the light bomber which they supplanted, the old Hind biplane, the Blenheim carrying twice the weight of bombs eighty miles an hour faster for three times the distance. These aircraft were being crated up and sent to Egypt by sea.

It was realised that they were capable of flying out to Egypt in a series of hops, and as they were bombers the obvious people to do this were crews from Bomber Command. The story circulating was that Bomber Command pilots did not like flying over the sea – and there was an element of truth in this, many of them who had to fly to Aldergrove in Northern Ireland automatically opting for the shortest sea crossing by flying up to Stranraer before launching themselves across the twenty-five miles of the Great Unknown to Larne. A bright staff officer in Coastal Command, they said, heard of this, and explained that navigating over water was an everyday occurrence to his crews, so the operation was handed over to Coastal Command *in toto*. As well as getting the aircraft out to Egypt quicker the operation would give the ferry pilots the opportunity of flying a modern aircraft, with all its technical advances.

So a Blenheim Delivery Flight organisation was set up at Thorney Island, near Portsmouth, with dual-control Blenheims and a couple of instructors. Three crews at a time were drawn from the squadrons and detached to Thorney Island. As was standard practice in Coastal Command, each Blenheim would have two pilot/navigators and a wireless operator, and a fourth crew member – a fitter, rigger or electrician – would ensure the serviceability of engines and airframes. Competition to get on the flights was intense but, eventually, my name came up.

No. 10 Blenheim Delivery Flight formed at Thorney Island on 10 May 1939, with Squadron Leader Abraham in command, and we started our conversion course without delay. The Mark 1 Blenheim was our first experience of modern-generation aircraft and we were very impressed with them. Of all-metal construction, they had two 840 horsepower engines and all the latest hydraulics – undercarriage, flaps, gun turret and variable-pitch airscrews. They also had the latest altimeter, which had three fingers instead of the single one on our Ansons. The large, medium and small concentric fingers were arranged like a clock, and it looked like a clock for much of the time as the small finger was hidden until one got to a fair altitude. This was to have a bearing on the subsequent navigation. From the pilot's seat the big Mercury engines, two and a half times as powerful as those in our Ansons, obstructed much of the sideways view, and all of the wings. The nose was short and fell away rapidly. The general impression, as you sat right up in the front, was that the Blenheim consisted merely of the two big engines stuck out on the end of the wing roots – the wings and tail were invisible.

The Blenheim also introduced us to the Shadow Factory. Hitherto all aircraft had been built by the old established manufacturers, but they could no longer cope with the rush of orders resulting from the RAF's expansion, and the work was farmed out to other engineering firms, who built brand-new factories for the job, called Shadow Factories.

'Hey, come and look at this!' said Goode of 206 Squadron, sticking his head out through the cockpit roof of his aircraft.

'What's up?'

He pointed to a metal plate riveted to the instrument panel.

'Blenheim Mark One. Airframe No. 684388. Engine Nos. 6H/7593 and 6H/8142. Austin Motor Company, Birmingham.'

'*Austins*! They make Austin Sevens, not bloody aeroplanes! What's wrong with Bristol's? They designed the darned things.'

We carried the bad news elsewhere.

'Grow up, chaps,' said Worthington, 'Austins have been making these things for six months and there hasn't been a single accident on the BDFs since they started. You'll get used to it.'

Which we did.

Squadron Leader Abraham called a conference.

'Egypt will be getting pretty warm by now, so you'll all need khaki tropical kit. Sergeant Pilots and Airmen will draw theirs from Main Stores tomorrow but officers, of course, have to provide their own.

You'd all better nip in to Gieves's branch in Pompey and get it, at least two of each garment.'

That was bad news. Just how much that lot was going to cost us we hadn't yet worked out. Even worse news was to follow as Abraham continued.

'Previous BDFs have taken three days to get to Egypt, but we will do it in two, lunching at Marseille and going on to Malta for the night. I want all compasses swung* and all front guns harmonised.†️ Six ammunition drums will be carried for each turret gun and these are to be in place for the compass swing, as are all engine spares, which are to be stowed between the spars. Edwards, you will carry these tasks on my aircraft as you are to be my navigator.'

I groaned. Silently, of course.

'At the end of each day I want a progress report from the two captains and Flying Officer Edwards as to the state of the three aircraft. Now get cracking.'

We dismissed, the sergeant pilots having one thing on their minds: the disappointment of having to get to Egypt in two days, instead of three. The officers had a second thing to think about: the cost of their tropical kits. *I* had a third thing on my mind: the responsibility for navigating the entire flight. There was disenchantment, even incipient mutiny, in the air.

'Whoever heard of getting to Egypt in two days,' said Humpherson indignantly. 'Everybody else has taken three over it, and spent the night in Marseille. The French Air Force take us to really sleazy joints, you know.'

I hadn't heard that one, but I'd heard Abraham tell us to buy tropical kit.

* The magnetic poles of the earth are not in the same position as the geographical poles. They also alter their position from year to year, so the compass needle rarely points in the correct direction. The difference between true north and magnetic north is known as 'variation'. The metal parts of the aircraft also have an effect on the compass, which is called 'deviation'. Both these have to be taken into account in navigation, so each month the aircraft compass was 'swung' using a tripod-mounted external compass as reference.

† The fixed, forward-firing guns can never be mounted near the gunsight, which has to be in front of the pilot's eyes. In the case of the Blenheim it was an astonishing fifteen feet away in the wing. Harmonising involved adjusting the gun mounting and gunsight so that they converged at 200 yards, our customary fighting range.

'It's a damned swizz, making us buy our own khaki in order to deliver the King's aircraft to Egypt. We should be issued with it, like the airmen. I don't think I can afford it.'

Some people had had the foresight to borrow tropical kit from other pilots in their squadrons who had been overseas, but those of us who hadn't voted for mutiny. We bought nothing, and said nothing about it. We'd sweat it out in Egypt in our blues.

'About this two-day nonsense,' said Goode. 'My Flight Commander was on a previous trip, and he said that the CO is taken to the Senior Officers' Mess for lunch at Marseille but we go to a junior mess. And they give you lots of wine. Let's get stuck into the vino; if we're sozzled at the end of lunch Abraham wouldn't dare let us fly. Then we can sober up for the evening's entertainment.'

'Now, that's an idea,' said someone. 'I'll have a word with the sergeants to see if they'll fall in with it.'

The plan for spreading the mutiny was agreed all round.

The Blenheims were not fully operational, as some of their equipment was to be fitted after their arrival in Egypt. On our flight only the lead aircraft would carry a wireless set, so there could be no communication between the three machines, as even the Aldis signalling lamps were not available. Indeed, there was no intercom between crew members even. The pilot and navigator were stuck up in the nose, and we carried so much in the way of tools and engine spares, which could only be accommodated between the spars, that we were cut off from the wireless operator and fourth crew member in the back. We eventually rigged up a crude endless string device, to which we tied messages and fed them inch by inch between back and front of the aircraft. This sort of situation was not uncommon at a time when our factories were still struggling to catch up in the armament race; witness the fact that 23 Squadron's Hurricanes were not fitted with variable-pitch airscrews.

We got away from Thorney Island at 0735 on 24 May and set course for Lyon, from where we were to turn south down the Rhône valley for Marseille. We flew into ten-tenths cloud over France and were forced up to 8,000 feet where, in typical pre-war fashion, our single radio set packed up. I told Squadron Leader Abraham to turn south on an estimated turning time, and we eventually flew clear of cloud, but I was now hopelessly lost. Not a single feature on the ground could be related to anything on my map. Abraham, a confirmed Francophile, stopped humming an Edith Piaf song and asked for our position. I couldn't give it him. 'Well, hurry up and find yourself, we're getting through the petrol, you know.'

By the time he'd finished 'Sur le pont d'Avignon' I was still lost, and getting anxious, as was Abraham.

'Get a bearing from Marignane.'

'Can't, sir, the wireless is on the blink.'

As we spoke No. 2 slid into very close formation, and the navigator mouthed sweet nothings, and waved his arms about.

'That chap's either barmy, or he knows where we are and is trying to tell us something,' said Abraham. 'Let's go over the navigation together. If we can't sort it out we'll let number two take over the lead. Give me your log.' He went through it point by point. 'Hmm, yes. Well the first leg was okay, we hit the French coast spot on. Now how long did you fly the south-easterly course? This looks odd. Is your watch all right?'

'I wasn't using my watch, sir, I was using the dashboard clock.'

'Well, that's accurate enough, but it doesn't tie in with your logged times. You sure you used that clock?'

'Yes, sir, there it is,' I cried, pointing to it.

'Clock, man. CLOCK! That's the bloody altimeter!'

Oh, my God! So it was. On that damned, new-fangled instrument 7,000 feet looked like nine o'clock, my approximate time for changing course. I started to repair the damage, and eventually found the error.

'Well, Edwards, you turned south too early, didn't you. *How* early?

I quailed as I gave him the answer.

'Forty-three minutes! FORTY-THREE! *Nobody* makes that amount of error. So where are we?'

'A hundred and thirty miles west of track, sir, and off our maps.'

'Well, this must be the Massif Centrale,' said Abraham. 'Somewhere round Clermont-Ferrand.'

'Sorry, sir, it's still not on the map. But if we carry on south we'll hit the Mediterranean coast, then we can just turn left for Marseille.'

'Hasn't it struck you, Edwards, that we may be so far west that we won't hit the French coast at all. That we could fly straight into Spain where, you may remember, there's a civil war going on. Would you prefer to be attacked by a Fiat CR42 or by one of these new fancy jobs of Hitler's, the Messerschmitt 109?'

'In that case, sir, steer ten degrees to port.'

'I'm making it twenty degrees, Edwards. I'm not having my arse blown off by a trigger-happy Nazi.'

'Perish the thought, sir. Twenty degrees to port it is. I'll log it as from now.'

'Do that. But do put in the correct time, there's a good chap. It's ten-fifteen, Edwards, not eight thousand two hundred and fifty bloody feet.'

We clawed our way back on to the map, closed up into a really tight formation over Marignane to let the French Air Force know how good we were, and landed after four hours in the air.

I have sometimes regretted that we found ourselves so soon, as we had been heading for Barcelona, and would have arrived just in time for Franco's victory parade that day, which included a fly-past of aircraft. To have had three neutral RAF Blenheims in the parade would have caused an international row of such gigantic proportions that it was the sort of black show that, however horrifying the punishment at the time, in the long run might have done one a lot of good. You know the sort of thing – 'Remember Dopey Edwards? Led a formation of Blenheims into Franco's victory parade in 1939. *Hell* of a black, the Foreign Secretary nearly had to resign over it. Tells a jolly good story about it when he's had a couple. He'd be a real asset to the Squadron, sir. I think we ought to have him.'

I set the refuelling of the aircraft in motion, confirmed the mutiny with the sergeant pilots and went off to get stuck into the vino in the junior officers' mess.

When the CO returned from his lunch he was greeted by five simpering pilots, and we thought we'd won. But we hadn't reckoned on his determination. He drove us like a flock of giggling geese to our aircraft, and we climbed in.

115

'What's that?' said Abraham as I slid into the cockpit alongside him.

'The altimeter, sir.'

'And that?'

'The clock, sir.'

'Correct. Now Malta's a small island, so you *will* get us there in one, won't you?'

We flew just east of south, five thousand feet above the blueness of the Mediterranean, which was flecked from horizon to horizon with the white horses blown up by the fresh north-westerly wind that was speeding our passage, and turned left round the San Antioco promontory in Sardinia. Now on a south-easterly course, and with the wind right behind us, we sped along at over 220 knots. And the wireless was working again. Keeping well to the north of Pantellaria, as Italy was a potential enemy if war came, we continued on the last leg of our flight to Malta. I took a drift every ten minutes, correcting the course as necessary, and sat contentedly back, quite glad that Abraham was doing the flying, and not me. It was far more fun looking down at that sea a mile below us, the sea the Phoenicians had sailed those hundreds of years ago. Who knew, perhaps we were flying over the site of Atlantis? Maybe, hundreds of feet below that sea, were the foundations and shards that were all that would remain of a civilisation that would never, in their wildest dreams, have visualised men flying at 250 miles an hour over their land. But flying we were, and a very relaxing existence it was.

Then, just to the right of Atlantis, the horizon took on a more defined form, the haziness became more dense. The months of training at Thorney Island registered. It was ships, and naval ships at that. I took a bearing on them and worked out their position. I didn't draw Abraham's attention to them yet as I wanted to present him with a *fait accompli*, to impress him and make up for my morning's gaffe. As we drew nearer, the ships materialising out of the haze revealed themselves to be Italian, and a complete battle fleet. I made my notes, then tapped Abraham on the sleeve.

'Italian battle fleet, sir, bearing green zero-four-zero degrees.'

'They're naval ships all right. Sure they're Italian?'

'Quite sure, sir. Four battleships, nine cruisers, twelve destroyers and some odds and ends. If you'll fly round them I'll get an accurate course and speed and more ship details.'

'All right, but I won't buzz them too close. What with Abyssinia and all that we're not exactly the best of friends.'

I got the initial details which I wanted and passed a message to the wireless operator on our string-operated intercom: 'To Headquarters, Middle East Command, Cairo; repeated HQ Coastal Command, Lee-on-Solent. From No. 10 BDF in transit Malta – Mersah Matruh. Italian battle fleet at sea position 13 degrees 15 minutes East, 37 degrees 18 minutes North. Course 315 degrees true, speed 18 knots. Composition 4 battleships, 9 cruisers, 12 destroyers, 11 others. Amplification follows. 1740 hours, 25/5/39. Ends.' As Abraham continued to circle the ships I got down to the detail of the amplifying report: 'Further to my signal of 1740 hours battleships are one Littorio class, 3 Cavour. Heavy cruisers 3 Zara, 2 Trento. Light cruisers 2 Condottieri Type C, 2 Type D. Destroyers, 7 Navigatori, 5 Aviere. 11 others. Course now 275 degrees true. Ends.'

With my job now finished I could relax and appreciate the beauty of this great battle fleet, ranging from the 35,000-ton leviathans down to the darting fifteen-hundred-ton destroyers, all rising and falling, lifting and rolling to the rhythm of their individual types, the fast destroyers thrusting their way through the seas in rapid oscillation, the cruisers taking the thing in a more leisurely and dignified way, and the massive battleships in slow, ponderous and enormously impressive style. We climbed away.

'Course for Malta please, Edwards.'

'One-four-two degrees magnetic sir. ETA eighteen forty-two hours.'

By 1837 Malta and Gozo rose out of the haze, and we landed at the rather small aerodrome of Hal Far, Abraham cramming on his brakes as soon as we hit the deck. There was just time to get the aircraft refuelled and hangared, and the met forecast ordered for the morning, before dashing off to the mess for dinner.

The inhabitants of the mess at Hal Far were an interesting mixture of RAF and Fleet Air Arm, all of them flying obsolete biplanes. Down at Kalafrana were moored the Scapa flying boats of 202 Squadron, the pilots living here at Hal Far, and an assortment

117

of anti-aircraft co-operation and meteorology units were dotted round. The Navy had a variety of aircraft, including the Walruses and Swordfish, the latter to do such sterling work in the war to come, and their pilots to face such appalling odds in them.

'Now, don't forget, chaps, tropical kit in the morning,' said Abraham as we said goodnight.

CHAPTER 9

SERIOUS TIMES AHEAD

braham wasn't at all pleased to see the mixture of khaki and blues that his officers wore as they assembled for the onward flight, but there was nothing he could do about it, except to express his disapproval, which he did. He went on to say, 'Now don't forget, everybody, if you have engine trouble, or any other disaster, and think you can't make it to Egypt then you can force-land in Libya. But only if you really have to. You're going to be mighty unpopular if you hand over our latest light bomber for Mussolini's gang to examine.'

We got airborne just after 0900 and set off on the four-hour flight to Mersah Matruh, on the north coast of Egypt. Having cleared Libya safely we altered course to starboard until we reached the Egyptian coast, then slipped inland and flew eastwards over that harsh and impressive landscape – yellow sand and rock stretching out for miles ahead, and to the south of us. The beaches were of very light sand, almost white, and the colour of the sea ranged from deep blue to very pale, depending on its depth, the shallows being edged by whiter-than-white surf for as far as the eye could see.

Mersah Matruh, when we reached it, was an advanced landing ground with few facilities and no mess, so we were refuelled from four-gallon petrol tins by an Arab crew under an RAF NCO, a laborious business taking a couple of hours. But a very welcome couple of hours they were. As soon as we were sure the refuelling was in swing we borrowed the NCO's fifteen hundredweight truck, drove to a wonderful beach where we were the only people, peeled off and swam. After drying out in the sun we dressed and went to the only hotel, and lay in long lounging chairs, awaiting lunch. Delicious oriental smells were drifting from the kitchen.

'There's only one thing missing to complete the picture, chaps,' I said. 'It's rough luck on you lot, but I'm only navigating. I'm having a pint of Pimms Number One.'

The other two pilots looked uneasily at Squadron Leader Abraham, who was lying alongside, eyes contentedly closed. He spoke.

'Well, special occasion. Half a pint for the pilots and a pint apiece for the navigators. On me.'

They arrived, and Abraham gave the toast, his own particular brand that we had become so used to in our fortnight's acquaintanceship – 'Cheers frightfully ho, chaps.'

'Cheers frightfully ho, sir.'

'Gosh,' I thought to myself, 'can *anything* equal this as a style of living?'

We got airborne again for the easy overland run to Ismailia and, as the villages and promontories ran under our wing, I ticked them off – Sidi Haneish, Ras el Hikmak, El Alamein. At Zagazig I said, 'Bradshaw* to Ismailia now, sir. ETA seventeen-eleven.'

I relaxed as we flew eastwards along the railway line, passing the pyramids to our left until, in the distance, the silvery streak of the Suez Canal showed up. Nos. 2 and 3 tucked their wings into a tight V formation, Abraham went to full throttle, and dived in a low sweep over the airfield, pulling up into a sharp climb before waving the two wing men away in a Prince of Wales feathers, a manoeuvre strictly forbidden by those in authority, but indulged in by most as long as it didn't put other aircraft at risk.

We landed. The late afternoon sun was pleasantly warm, and no problem for those of us in our rebellious blues, though we did look a bit odd.

'Congratulations all round,' said Abraham. 'We've done the UK to Egypt in thirty-three hours, the fastest ever. We've knocked Imperial Airways' record for six.'

The mess buildings were single-storey and spacious, the quarters equally so, and simply furnished. All the windows were open and

---

* Bradshaw was the railway guide. In those days railway stations had their names in foot-high white lettering on black boards. It was standard practice, when lost, to come down low and read the name, following the line to your destination if you felt like it.

the curtains stirred gently in the dying evening breeze. As I lay outstretched in an easy chair a faint padding noise preceded the appearance of my bearer in his uniform of red fez and white gaballieh, gathered at the waist with a belt in the colours of the RAF. He suggested that it was time for my shower and I returned from it to find him searching helplessly through my suitcase for the slightest trace of khaki drill. I explained, with minimal undermining of the authority of the British Raj, that not all English Milords' finances ran to such luxuries. Goode and Anderson would, no doubt, be spinning similar tales. I joined them, and the three of us braved the disapproval of the senior officers as we entered the mess together. We brought fresh news from home, however, and our blues were soon forgotten in the discussions of the worsening situation in Europe, and the new types of aircraft coming off the production lines to replace the obsolescent stuff that many of us still flew.

In the Middle East the day started early, before the sun got too hot for comfort. As we walked down to Flights to hand over our Blenheims the sights and sounds were different from those of England. The character of the light at six in the morning had an ethereal, unreal quality, as though viewed through a veil. The colours, against the background of the all-pervading sand, were suffused with pink, the mop-heads of the palm trees standing out in an atmosphere clearer than that of the rose pink in which their trunks were bathed. The aircraft, in their sandy desert camouflage, looked foreign to us, though right for their purpose. Sounds were muted. And it was still cool.

We now had the task of handing over our aircraft which I, in my innocence, had thought would be a familiarisation flight for one of the Squadron pilots. I'd planned a Cook's tour of the neighbourhood, starting with a flight the length of the Suez Canal, then over Cairo and back via the pyramids. Alas, it was to be a much more mundane business, entailing interminable checking of every item fitted to the airframe by the manufacturers. There would be, for example: sockets, jack, four-contact, Ref. 37B/4738/18, Qty 6.

With one Flying Officer Jacques riding shotgun on me, as he was to sign for the aircraft, I'd found five of them.

121

'Look, old boy, the other one will be here somewhere; we can take it for granted,' I said.

'Not on your Nellie,' said Jacques. 'You're off to the UK in a couple of days and *I'm* not going to be stuck paying for it.'

'Well, I don't know where the damned thing is.'

'Tough.'

'All right, stick it on the deficiency list with the rest of the stuff.'

'Willdo.'

The rose-pink ethereality of the early morning air had disappeared as the temperature rose. The inside of the Blenheim was now like an oven, and we both came out for air. Leading Aircraftman Willard, my wireless operator, was walking past and I hailed him over.

'Look, Willard, I can't find these items, and some are obviously electrical. See if you can find them, and show Mr Jacques.'

Jacques and Willard disappeared into the aircraft and a variety of noises indicated their passage up and down its length, many of them being muffled curses as they struggled over the wing spars, and hit their heads and shins on things. When they reappeared Willard had done a good job, as the list of deficiencies had come down to five.

'I'll just go and see the Flight Sergeant, sir,' he said. 'He'll know where the rest of the equipment is.'

He winked as he went away, and Jacques and I sat under the wing. It wasn't much cooler there, but it was certainly better than sweating it out in the winter woollies that I was togged up in.

In a quarter of an hour Willard, his side pocket bulging, returned with Flight Sergeant Jesmond, our engine fitter, in tow. As Willard climbed back into the Blenheim he hissed, 'Nicked 'em from the wireless section, sir.'

'Regarding this deficiency list, Mr Jacques,' said Jesmond, 'I've told Willard where the remaining electrical equipment is – he'll show you in a minute.'

Willard's head appeared out of the turret hatch.

'If you'll come in now, sir, I think you'll find the electrical equipment is all here.'

After the usual scuffles and bumps Jacques ticked them off his list.

'But there are still these two – he indicated items with a stores reference number as long as his forearm.'

'Ah, now those, sir. Yesss, er, actually, they're on the engines, sir. These items are so low-stressed that when we do an engine change they are transferred to the new engine, so they're listed as separate items. If you'll come with me, sir.'

He opened an access panel on the side of one of the engines and pointed into the gloomy interior of the nacelle. 'It's up there, sir, between the supercharger casing and the hydraulic oil pump. I've got a torch here. When you've found it you can check its reference.

Jacques put his arm in, felt around and withdrew it, distinctly oily.

'Can't really see it.'

'Ah, I don't think you've gone in far enough, sir. It's about another foot in.'

Jacques took a look at his arm, decided against further exploration, signed for the Blenheim, and left.

'Thanks, chaps, I'll buy you a drink on the boat.'

With the Blenheims handed over our official duties were finished and those of us in blues could now change into the civilian lightweight kit that we'd brought with us.

For the three days before we joined our ship at Port Said we had been made honorary members of the French Club on the banks of the Suez Canal. As, on the second day, we lay there under the palms in lounging chairs, Anderson said, 'There's our tub.' Coming north up the canal was the three-funnelled *Narkunda*, the 20,000-ton P&O ship on which we were to travel from Port Said to Marseille.

'Funny things, funnels,' said an old Middle East hand lying alongside us, 'and very important out here, especially round the Persian Gulf. The Navy used to keep the peace out there with an old three-funnelled cruiser, a clapped-out pre-war ship which used to loose off a few rounds in coastal areas when various people were getting a bit uppity. Then the Admiralty replaced her with a more modern ship. But it only had two funnels, and they found that the locals weren't at all impressed – funnels were more important to them than guns. This ship hadn't half the deterrent effect – local uprisings increased. So they brought back the old three-piper again.'

Narkunda's hull stood so high above the banks of the canal that it looked as though she was gliding along through a sea of sand. We waved to her passengers as they slipped slowly past the end of the garden; we would be joining them next day at Port Said.

In the meantime I had a job to do. I'd bought a bolt of silk to be made up into shirts when I got home, and didn't want to pay the import duty on it. I took my parachute to the parachute section, pulled the rip cord, and got them to repack it with my silk inside, making a strong mental note to remember to unpack it when I got home. I didn't want to go hurtling to my death wrapped in shirting material if I baled out of my aircraft.

That evening we travelled up to Port Said, and as we were now getting low on cash we came to an arrangement with the hotelier, cancelling our rooms, staying up all night and spending our money on a round of clubs and belly dancers. At six in the morning we dismissed our taxi and sat on our suitcases on the quayside. Out in the bay the great ship that was to take us home floated insubstantially in the vapours of a sea mist, rose red in the rising sun. It was cool, but with the certainty of great heat to come. Slowly, as the sun rose higher, it burned the colours away, and *Narkunda* emerged from the mirage. Soon, gallabieh'd porters appeared, followed by streams of taxis disgorging other passengers, and tenders left the ship's side to embark us.

Narkunda had come from Australia, via Singapore, Bombay and Suez and had the usual complement of passengers, rich Australians coming to have a look at the 'old country', planters from Singapore, Indian Army and RAF from Bombay, and the Sudan Civil Service who would have boarded at Suez. The P&O was the major lifeline of the British Raj, a national institution, running up to Hong Kong as well. Although Imperial Airways had extended their Middle and Far East services with flying boats and Handley Page 42s, so that they could now fly you to India within the week, it was still the Peninsular and Oriental Steam Navigation Company which carried the vast bulk of the Empire's servicemen, administrators, and their families. The P&O had even invaded the language, the word 'posh' having been introduced by them to apply to their passengers. In those days, before air conditioning, the forced draught ventilation system on ships was only of limited use – if it wasn't too hot then the additional breeze was refreshingly welcome. But once the ship reached the burning heat of the tropics, all it did was to blast the hot ambient air to make a furnace of the cabin. The coolest cabins were those away from the sun, the port side ones on the outward voyage and the starboard ones when coming home. So the experienced traveller specified, when making reservations, 'Port outward, starboard home', shortened by the booking clerks to POSH.

As travel was an expensive business the word posh became associated with the rich, so changed its application slightly. As officers we travelled first class, and it wasn't half as much fun as we had expected, as by our standards the passengers were on the old and stodgy side. Many had been forced by financial circumstances into the colonial life, as only there could they attain a living standard comparable with their more fortunate peers at home. Or it may have been a streak of romanticism in their make-up. To the youngsters of our day the heroes were almost entirely single-minded upholders of the outposts of the Empire, the defenders of the Raj. They fought gallantly, putting death before dishonour. And, of course, they played the game! But in their restricted, frequently lonely, communities, matters that might appear trifles elsewhere became of much importance. The social pecking order could be of depressing rigidity, and there was a pronounced lack of originality, both in thought and action. They lost their children early when they were sent home to prep school in England, to live with aunts and grandparents for years at a time.

In England, due to the slaughter of their menfolk in the Great War, there were far more women than men at this time, and the 'fishing fleets' of surplus young women made the voyage east to hunt for husbands under a tropical moon. The unsuccessful ones came home as 'returned empties'. It was all rather sad. Many of the wives lacked the mental resources to fill the too-empty days resulting from the absence of their children and the surfeit of servants. An inevitable increase in extra-marital activities went with the excessive leisure, but basically they were quite Victorian in their principles. Many of the men would retire early through the ravages of life in a hot climate, and would find impecunious retirement in Cheltenham to be a bewildering affair, with no servants, and the accelerated pace of life and deterioration of manners. Some of the men drank more than was advisable. It may have been patronising of me, but I felt a great deal of sympathy for them. The British Empire was underpinned by a great deal of hidden human suffering and sacrifice. They all thought that Hitler was a bit of a bounder.

We found it to be more fun in the tourist class, and had the best of both worlds, first class passengers being allowed down into the tourist decks. Tourists were not allowed to come up to the first class accommodation, of course, but the occasional shilling to the stewards ensured a steady stream of selected popsies up the forbidden companionways, and we got many an envious glance from colonels' daughters, imprisoned with their parents the other side of the lounge, together with an equal number of disapproving ones from their parents because of the row we were kicking up. We lazed the days away until we docked at Marseille, my first impression of that port, which I had looked down at so thankfully after my navigation gaffe a few days before, being the wave of garlic fumes as the blue-clad porters swarmed up the gangways to fight over our luggage.

We said goodbye to our voyage companions, who were continuing their trip home for another week via Gibraltar, and left *Narkunda* for sleepers on the Paris–Dover train, and so on to Victoria, where the twelve members of No. 10 Delivery Flight dispersed to their various units. I took the *Flying Scotsman* northwards and arrived back in 233 Squadron on 5 June, flat broke but happy.

I awoke the next morning and lay late abed, reliving the trip to Egypt and thinking that there were far worse ways of earning a living. In a few hours the bar would open, and the traditional Leuchars Sunday lunchtime would start with the Pimms No. 1 to which many of us had become addicted. The door was flung open and Ali Barber appeared, noisily as usual.

'Want to fly, Dopey?' he roared in his customary whisper.

'On a Sunday! Not particularly.'

'Look, I'm in a bit of a spot. Some Army officers have been promised a trip to look at the camouflage of their anti-aircraft guns and the arrangements have been mucked up.'

'By whom, Ali?'

'Oh, all right. Maybe I slipped up a bit. Anyway, they're here now, and the CO says to take the first aircraft in the hangar and get airborne as soon as possible. Now, what do you think?'

'I was thinking of that belly dancer in Ismailia.'

'Well you can't do anything about that now. Look, we can't let the Army down. The CO says we've got to fly two pilots: don't want to kill the buggers, do we?'

'Oh, all right. Toss.'

Ali lost, so I would fly the aircraft down to Usworth and he would fly it back. As we loaded up the three Army officers I said to Ali, 'You realise that this is the CO's machine?' (The brass ignition switches were polished bright, naval fashion.)

'It's okay, he said to take the first one out of the hangar.'

I flew down the coast, did a trip round the gun sites and landed at Usworth, where I did a mild overshoot, but nothing to worry about, and certainly not meriting the audible criticism of Ali, who went on to explain to the Army that, on our return to Leuchars, he would show them just how short you could land an Anson. 'You can put them down on a pocket handkerchief if you really try,' he concluded. Considering that I'd helped him out of a hole he was being mighty ungrateful.

In good weather the navigator on a coast crawl can do as little, or as much, work as he feels like. I read the Sunday papers, knowing that even Ali could find Leuchars. Eventually, he asked one of the gunners to wind down the undercarriage, and then throttled back for the landing, from then on giving a running commentary to his rapt audience. On glancing up from my paper I was surprised to have to look *up* at a tree, as we were still a fair way from the aerodrome, but assumed that Ali knew what he was doing, so went back to the love-nest slaying so gorily depicted in my paper.

'You see,' Ali was bellowing, 'you can gun these things in semi-stalled, just hanging on the engines like this.'

A look at the tell-tale airspeed indicator above my navigation table gave me the impression that we were nearer ninety per cent stalled.

'Then, as you come to the leeward hedge, you chop the throttles, so,' continued the maestro.

The leeward boundary of the aerodrome was a six-foot-deep drainage ditch, and we hit the far edge of it with a tooth-jarring crash. The plywood surface of the port wing burst open, and the whole of the landing gear on that side was rammed upwards through the wreckage, followed by the yellow enormity of the inflating emergency dinghy. The impact flung us into the air and, before we hit the deck again, one of the Army officers leaned across, pointed to the scene of devastation and said, 'Is that usual?' I hadn't got the time to say that there *were* other ways of landing an aircraft, so I yelled 'Hang on' to him. We arrived for our second landing, and spun and jolted our creaking and protesting way on starboard wheel, the tail wheel and a rapidly disintegrating port wing tip.

As the dust settled I couldn't help observing, as Ali had been so poisonous about my landing at Usworth, that had *I* been demonstrating such an unusual landing no power on earth would have persuaded me to use the CO's aircraft for it. From the front of the now silent aircraft a great groan arose from Ali as the full hideousness of his crime sank in, not helped by my reminder that we were both due at the CO's cocktail party that night.

'Don't worry,' blustered Ali, 'I'll wait till he's had a couple before I break the news.'

'I'm not worrying, Ali. It's nothing to do with me.'

The party was an undoubted success, many of the local people having been invited, including Jane and her parents, the vicar, half the committee of the Royal and Ancient Golf Club and many of the Baillies of the town. The whisky and gin flowed and an air of bonhomie reigned.

'Ah, Dopey!' said the CO. 'Have a good trip to Usworth today?'

'Yes sir. I think we gave the Ack-Ack gunners what they wanted.'

Ali now joined us, having screwed up his courage by matching Louis about two to one in gins.

'Ah, Barber, you were on the trip too, weren't you. Any problems?'

'Well, sir, we had a little trouble with the undercarriage on landing here. Port side sort of collapsed.'

'Oh, dear,' said Louis. 'Much damage?'

'Oh, I think a new landing gear on that side will do the trick, sir.'

'A *completely* new landing gear? How did it happen?'

'I hit the leeward ditch as we landed, sir, and it pushed the port gear up through the wing.'

'Up through the wing! So what other damage has been done?'

'Well, sir, perhaps a few repairs to the main spar and the top surface of the wing. And it may be advisable to have the engine mountings trued up.'

As the list grew the smile faded from Louis's face. However, it was a public party and he kept control over himself.

'Oh, dear, Barber. What aircraft was this?'

'Q, sir,' quavered Ali.

'Q?' breathed Louis, far too quietly. 'KEWWWWWW?' he bellowed in a conversation-stopper. 'My own bloody Q?'

The parson looked embarrassed, and guests examined their glasses minutely. His wife leapt into the breach.

'Louis, dear, have you met Baillie McIntyre yet?'

'No, I haven't,' roared Louis, ignoring the Baillie. 'Do you realise what this young pup has done? He's wrecked my ruddy aircraft.' He turned on Ali. 'Get out of my house, you ham-fisted oaf.' Ali shot towards the door. 'Just get out, you moron,' pursuing him into the darkness. 'I'll see you in the morning, Barber. Oh yes, I'll see you in the morning, my friend!'

But Ali had the devil's luck. Louis had to go away first thing and Ali's posting to a flying boat squadron at Calshot came through. He performed a miracle, and got cleared by both squadron and station in one day.

'Clearing' was a lengthy process whereby you had to go round every department and obtain a signature that you did not have any outstanding debts or, if you had them, you signed acknowledging your liability. You waded through Flight Commander, Flight Stores, Squadron Stores, Squadron Commander, Navigation, Signals and

Parachute officers, Accounts, Armoury and so on *ad nauseam*. It normally took about three days but Ali did it in one, and must have worked a miracle to do so without getting Louis's actual signature. He packed his bags and hopped on the next train to Calshot. Louis, baulked of his prey on his return, took it out on the Adjutant for a while and then settled down.

There was a sequel to the story in that, about two months later, Louis was promoted to Group Captain and sent to command Calshot. Ali later described it to me.

'It was Sunday morning and I was reading the paper in the anteroom when something made me look up. Towering over the top of the paper was the only hooked nose like it in the RAF. "Jesus," I thought, "he's come all this way just to get me just for pranging his bloody Anson."

"Ali," said Louis, "I don't wish to ruin your Sunday morning, but if you ever knock the bottom out of one of my flying boats, I'll have your guts for garters. Savvy?"

'We got on quite well again after that,' concluded Ali.

About a week after Ali's affair there was a distinct fillip to my morale. While still the youngest pilot in the Squadron I had now been promoted to Flying Officer, had clocked up over 600 hours and had flown more types of aircraft than any other junior officer due to my habit of scrounging whenever I saw an aircraft that wasn't in my logbook. Two new boys had arrived from their flying training school and I was given the task of giving them dual instruction to convert them on to Ansons. I was starting to acquire status. And I made sure that they knew what a retractable undercarriage was.

With the international situation degenerating at an ever-increasing rate the ferrying of Blenheims to the Middle East was accelerated by training no more new crews. Those who had been before had to go again. Surprisingly, this wasn't popular as most of us had shot our financial bolts on the first trip, but my name came out of the hat, and off I went to Thorney Island again. An urgent phone call to Cox and King's produced only forty of the fifty pounds needed for complete enjoyment of the trip, and when you consider that a new Ford 8 cost only £100, you'll appreciate just what sacrifices a junior officer, under the regulations of those days, had to make to ferry the King's aircraft out to Egypt.

No. 18 Blenheim Delivery Flight assembled at Thorney Island, commanded by Squadron Leader Buxton. Not wishing to navigate again I dropped hints as to the mess I'd made of the previous flight, when we'd nearly ended up in Franco's victory parade at Barcelona. But Buxton called for all our flying logbooks and, after studying them, called me in.

'Edwards, I see you got to Ismailia in two days last time. That must have called for damned good navigation. And you didn't do too badly at Ten FTS either – one "Exceptional" assessment and one "Above Average". You will be my navigator.'

I saluted unhappily and left the office.

The work of organising the Flight went into its smooth routine, but we struck difficulty with spares for our Mercury engines. Buxton called me in to his office again.

'Get over to Tangmere, Edwards. Here's a list of the spares we need. The Gladiator squadron are very kindly transferring them to our charge. Have 'em back by lunchtime.'

He hadn't specified the mode of transport, obviously expecting me to use a Blenheim, but I'd had my eye on the old Vildebeest torpedo bombers of 22 Squadron. One of their Flight Commanders was sympathetic and told me to take one.

Biplanes were simple machines, and it didn't take much more than a minute to get the hang of the cockpit and engine-starting system before flying off to Tangmere. The Vildebeest moved through the air with a characteristic rustling noise at slightly under the ton. Fully laden with torpedo, it nearly went backwards in a moderate breeze, and got a dreadful hammering from the Japanese in Singapore a couple of years later. I collected the spares and floated back to Thorney.

Buxton had two good ideas: one of them was to take three days over the trip – we reckoned that he must have heard about the brothel that the French Air Force recommended; the other was that as the Middle East people had been so unstinting in their generosity to the previous delivery flights, we'd take out a firkin of English bitter beer for them, the six officers of the flight chipping in for it. The precious firkin was lodged between the wing spars of the lead aircraft, and No. 18 BDF slipped into the air at 0750 on 26 July, setting course for Lyon. This time I made no mistake in navigation, and we turned down the Rhône valley and landed at Marignane three and a half hours later, a good half hour less than the time when we'd wandered over the Massif Centrale and French Catalonia on No. 10 BDF.

The French Air Force were, as ever, hospitable, sales being brisk on the Canabière that night, and the next morning we had an equally pleasant flight to Malta. After seeing the beer put into a cold room for the night we had a snack, followed by an afternoon's swimming at the flying boat base at Kalafrana, and a pleasant evening in the mess at Hal Far. By 1000 next day we'd got the beer aboard and flew at fairly high altitude across the Med to Mersah Matruh to keep it cool, and those of us who had no tropical kit were grateful for the warmth of our blues. The white sand beach at Mersah looked as delightful as ever, so as soon as we had stowed the firkin in the restaurant cool room we went down to the beach for a swim, this time suitably dressed in bathing trunks.

After lunch the Blenheims, as usual, were roastingly hot, so the firkin was rushed out at the last moment, and we got airborne for Heliopolis. Buxton agreed with my suggestion for routing ourselves to the south of the direct track, and an hour later we were circling the pyramids.

'Awful cads, those gunners of Napoleon,' said Buxton as we swept past the Sphinx. 'Shot the nose off that thing just for target practice, you know. Right, Edwards, course for Heliopolis, please.'

'Oh three two degrees magnetic, sir.'

We were very popular among the junior officers at Heliopolis when the word got round about our firkin, which was given two days to settle. Among the more senior officers, however, those of us who had no tropical kit were again the subject of disapproval as we sweated our way round in blue shirts with black ties, and thick blue trousers, especially as the trousers were designed to be brace-supported only, so tightening a belt around them left several inches of surplus material sticking up above the belt, an untidy arrangement. We also displayed no badges of rank. We were happier going around in pairs for mutual moral support, because we were damned if we were going to lash out yet more of our own money. But I *did* have the cream-coloured shirts which Gieves had made up for me from the silk which I'd smuggled back last time in my parachute, and that helped.

I handed over my aircraft with no snags this time, and on the third night a mess party was held, the firkin of beer being the guest of honour. It really had been an inspiration on Buxton's part, and the party went with a swing. I have a hazy recollection of an elderly Flight Lieutenant, thirty if he was a day – appearing at two in the morning, and bellowing that as far as he was concerned they could chuck every Blenheim ever built into the Suez canal if he had to put up with this sort of thing every time a bunch of clowns flew in a few more of them. Between times, we read the Cairo newspapers, which seemed to think, in those early August days, that the situation in Europe was getting even worse. Austria and Czechoslovakia had already been collected into Hitler's net. Now it looked as though Poland was due for the chop, and as far as we could gather we'd given Poland some guarantees.

Within the week we'd caught the next P&O boat back to Marseille, in this case the *Rawalpindi*. As we lounged on its decks with our gin slings not a soul on board would have given credence to the idea that in less than four months' time, the flaming hulk of this big ship would slide for ever into the cold depths of the Iceland Channel as Captain Kennedy took her into forlorn action against the overwhelming might of the battle cruiser *Scharnhorst*. Or that *Narkunda*, on which I'd made my previous return voyage, would be bombed to the bottom of the Atlantic off Casablanca.

As we didn't know, we didn't worry, and all too soon the voyage ended. Whereas I had arrived home from No. 10 BDF only flat broke, I was now horribly overdrawn, with a lingering suspicion that when all my Egyptian cheques came home to roost, my Cox and King's overdraft limit of forty pounds was going to be exceeded.

But all this was brushed aside, as Leuchars was seething with excitement: we were to re-equip with a new aircraft! Built by Lockheeds of Burbank, California, it was a military version of their fast Type 14 airliner, and was to be called the 'Hudson'. It was all-metal, had two 1,100 horsepower Cyclone engines, two fixed Browning guns firing forward and two more in a 360-degree rotation turret in the mid-upper position. It would carry 1,000 lb of bombs, had a top speed of 246 miles an hour, and unheard-of luxuries like an automatic pilot and an efficient cockpit heating system. This really was something – three times the horsepower, two and a half times the gun power, twice the range, five times the bomb load! There was only one snag: 224 Squadron were to get the Hudson first. *We* would have to wait.

With this aircraft we would be infinitely more efficient as a maritime reconnaissance squadron. Our principal task in the war that was now so obviously coming was the gathering of information on German shipping movements in the area of the North Sea between Scotland and Norway, and the attacking of that shipping. Our Ansons couldn't even *reach* Norway, and would leave an all-important gap unswept. If we *did* catch a ship our heaviest bomb was a pathetic one hundred pounder. But Ansons were what we would be starting the war with so, as Squadron Armament Officer, I had to get them on the top line. I supervised the checking of every aircraft's bombing and gunnery equipment, and that the bomb and ammunition storage was in order. When it was done I took the fortnight's leave that was due to me and went home to North Wales, by rail this time, as no aircraft could leave the station.

Tudor, my eldest brother, had joined the Territorial Army and was full of his two-pounder anti-tank guns. *Two* pounders, for God's sake. They'd bounce off the German armour from what I'd heard. He was also giving signs that he might want to transfer to the Air Force. We gassed about the services until our other brother, Teddy, chipped in. No militarist, almost a pacifist, he regarded us with a mixture of despair and tolerant amusement.

'You two really ought to stop playing toy soldiers,' he said. 'There's one sure thing, you're not getting *me* into a uniform, Hitler or no Hitler.'

Whatever plans we had, events overtook us, along with millions of others. Tudor *did* transfer to the RAF, to die in his Blenheim at Rotterdam, and Teddy *did* wear a uniform, surviving the Western Desert and Italy, only to die in his tank in Normandy after D-Day. It was good thing that we couldn't see into the future that late August day in 1939.

A telegram arrived, recalling me to my unit. I arrived back to find that we were officially mobilised for war. Surprisingly, my suggestion that I bomb up my Ansons and get our machine-guns loaded was turned down.

'You can't have a bunch of aircraft with fused bombs and loaded guns in a hangar,' I was told by the Station Adjutant.

'But they'll be dispersed all over the aerodrome, it'll be quite safe,' I pleaded.

'Now, calm down. We're not at war yet.'

'We damn well are, for all practical purposes.'

'Forget it. Anyway, if you did arm up, what on earth would we do with that explosive all over the shop when Hitler climbs down.'

'We can defuse the damn stuff.'

'Look, it's a perfectly plain order. No arming-up. Now do be a good chap and bugger off. I've got a lot of work to do.'

I gave up and went back to the mess, where two letters awaited me. The more interesting-looking one was from an Australian millionaire whom I'd flown illegally some months before. He'd remembered his promise – it was an invitation to a week's deerstalking on his estate, that wonderful tract of Perthshire that I'd flown him round. It would have been a great experience, but I would have to refuse. We were confined to the station.

I recognised the envelope of the other one. From Cox and King's, it read: 'Dear Mr Edwards, We note, with concern, the fact that the £40 overdraft facility which we granted to assist you in your second tour of duty in the Middle East has been exceeded, and that your overdraft now stands at £49–18–4. We trust that you will take immediate steps to reduce this to the agreed level.'

'Well, honestly,' I thought, 'not a single one of my aircraft armed up, and fifty pounds overdrawn at the bank. What a hell of a way to start a war!'

INDEX